'128'

THE STORY OF THE
ROYAL AIR FORCE CLUB

LONDON LAUGHS:
Royal Air Force Club, Piccadilly
"Do you often drop in for lunch?"

'128'

THE STORY OF THE ROYAL AIR FORCE CLUB

AIR COMMODORE HENRY PROBERT

WING COMMANDER MICHAEL GILBERT

ROYAL AIR FORCE CLUB
LONDON

First published in 2004 by
The Royal Air Force Club, 128 Piccadilly, London W1J 7PY
www.rafclub.org.uk

British Library Cataloguing in Publication Data:
a catalogue record for this book is available
from the British Library

ISBN 0-9547849-0-1

Produced for the Royal Air Force Club by
Bookplan Production Services and DAG Publications Ltd
Edited by Michael Boxall. Designed by David Gibbons

Printed and bound in Great Britain by
Creative Print and Design (Wales),
Ebbw Vale.

CONTENTS

LIST OF ILLUSTRATIONS

The Club has no pictorial record of interiors prior to the 1950s but does have portraits and photographs of some of the notable figures in its history. The aircraft illustrations are drawn from the Club's fine collection of original aviation paintings and are chosen to reflect the variety of aircraft that have featured in the history of the Royal Air Force over the years.

FOREWORD

BY

AIR CHIEF MARSHAL SIR LEWIS HODGES, KCB, CBE, DSO, DFC

I joined the Club in 1938, having been encouraged to do so, as we all were, on graduating from Cranwell. This was not many months before the outbreak of war, and for the next six years I had little opportunity to make use of the Club. However, on the few occasions when I was in London I made a point of calling in, when I observed how welcoming and busy it was, and I continued afterwards to appreciate it as an important part of the Air Force scenery. But by the 1960s it was apparent that the Club's fortunes were not looking good. Membership was declining, the finances were at a very low ebb, and I felt strongly that something had to be done. Others, particularly Neil Cameron, felt likewise and we came to lead what Freddie Sowrey was to call a 'Colonels' Revolt'. When I now read the full story of what we did, why we did it and what it led to, as related by Henry Probert and Michael Gilbert, I hope I can be forgiven for believing that our efforts were justified.

This book is of course about much more. It shows how the Club reacted over its first eighty years to the vast changes occurring in the world at large and more specifically in the Royal Air Force. It brings out the significance of the active interest shown by the Service's more recent leaders in contrast to most of their predecessors. It demonstrates the debt owed to the many Committee members who over the years have given their time in different ways to the direction of the Club's affairs – some of course more effectively than others. It reminds us of the immeasurable contributions of countless members of staff from Secretaries downwards. Perhaps of greatest value it enables us to appreciate the vision displayed by its most influential leaders, and especially Lord Cowdray – but for whom the RAF might well never have had an Officers' Club of its own.

I count myself highly privileged to have played some part in all this and am delighted that the story is at last on record.

PREFACE

The possibility of writing a Club History was first mentioned in 1968 but not followed up, and not until 1992 did it again surface in the Committee. The idea then was to publish one in 1997 to coincide with the 75th Anniversary of the opening of 128 Piccadilly, but this was soon found to be too short a time scale and the project was further deferred. In 1995, however, we Committee members started to examine it carefully.

It seemed to us that by now there was an interesting and important tale to be told. Neither we ourselves nor most of the Club's members really seemed to know much about its origins, including the influence of Lord Cowdray, and its development and activities between the wars, during the Second World War and afterwards. We knew relatively little about the revolution in the Club's affairs that had occurred in the 1960s, including the circumstances that had given rise to it. Even the story of the subsequent modernisation and its associated events, not least the purchase of the freehold of the building, was largely unknown to many. Certainly, we agreed, it was about time to research the subject properly and record it in print.

At this stage I felt fingers were beginning to point in my direction, both as an RAF historian and as a long-serving member of the Committee. It needed some thought. Still currently working on my biography of Bomber Harris, I would not be able to start for another couple of years; I should need to enlist yet again my wife Audrey's computer expertise; and I should require help with the research in the Club archives and elsewhere. In 1999, however, the decision was made and with the Committee's backing I asked in the Newsletter for volunteers willing to lend me a hand. The response was most encouraging and in due course I asked Wing Commander Michael Gilbert, another historian and a fellow member of the RAF Historical Society, to examine the Club archives which would inevitably provide the primary source material.

Michael proved to be an excellent choice. Not only did he start reading the various Committee Minute-Books and compiling detailed notes, but he also presented the material in analytical form. Moreover, though still having much else on his plate, he was able to devote several days a month to working on the archives at the Club and acquiring in-depth knowledge of them. So eventually, once I was able to begin the actual drafting and he was regularly feeding material to me, we became a most effective partnership. This led me to invite him to become co-author and he readily agreed.

Others too have lent a hand. Squadron Officer Ida Cole has drawn on her knowledge of some of the London libraries and other important archives in order to obtain much of the material on which the opening chapter is based. Squadron Leader Joe Davies has dug around in the Air Historical Branch, the Public Record Office (now the National Archives) and elsewhere to obtain necessary background information about the significant RAF personalities and some of the relevant events. His Honour Harold Wilson, a recently elected General Committee member, has helped by criticising the draft and also taking on some of the administrative work. Moreover the Club Secretary, Mr Peter Owen, and senior members of his staff, particularly Kathryn Cooper, the Assistant Club Secretary, have given us essential back-up in many ways. Julia Hamlyn too deserves special thanks for her efficient and good-humoured response to Michael Gilbert's many questions concerning membership and Club activities over the past twenty years.

Hardly surprisingly, we have suffered our disappointments. We certainly thought that our appeals for recollections from longer-serving members would elicit greater response than they did. We hoped for at least a few contributions, particularly copies of letters, about the pre-war and wartime years, but there was virtually nothing, and even the post-war years proved largely barren. Reliable oral recollections too have been scarce, though with additional time we might well have invited more former Committee members to unlock their memories. We did, however, have an invaluable discussion of the events of the 'Colonels' Revolt' with Sir Lewis Hodges, Sir Freddie Sowrey and the late Sir Ivor Broom – and we are particularly grateful to Sir Lewis for also writing the Foreword.

We had problems with some of the documentation. True the Minutes of the main Club Committees seemed to be reasonably complete, but they were not always as carefully organised and presented as we should have liked and – a fault of committee minutes in general – their summaries of discussions and decisions did not seem always to convey much of a 'feel' for what was actually going on. The greatest gap from the historian's point of view was the absence of ordinary correspondence files and the demi-official letters which can so often prove the most revealing sources in historical work of this kind. We were surprised to find gaps in some of the major documentation – for example some of the crucial letters that were sent out to members at the time of the Colonels' Revolt were missing. Most fortunately our appeal to members enabled us to fill these particular gaps and we warmly thank those who came to the rescue. It does not say much, however, for the state of the Club's archives in bygone days.

Today, however, the Club's records are much better maintained, and in writing this first edition of its History Michael and I very much hope that it will prompt some of our readers to offer their own comments and recollections, together maybe with relevant documents, in the hope that a second edition may eventually be able to take advantage of them. Perhaps the Club Centenary will provide a suitable occasion, and we should like to think that the Committee will appoint one of its longer-serving members to advise on the proper maintenance of the present-day archive and the acquisition of new material.

For now, we commend this book to our Club members, future as well as present, and, it is to be hoped, to a wider audience, including some of the numerous visitors who may wish to know a bit more about the Club which so many of them admire.

Henry Probert

CHAPTER 1

ORIGINS

The Royal Air Force Club is almost as old as the Royal Air Force itself. Founded in November 1918, it had its roots in the Royal Flying Corps Club which had been established at 13 Bruton Street (close to Berkeley Square) in January 1917, following the first Committee Meeting on 5 October 1916.

The key figure in these initial stages was a 42-year-old insurance director, Mr Walter Bersey, who put up the money and oversaw its affairs. Later, in 1917, he was to be commissioned as an equipment officer in order to help organise the large scale 'infusion of women' into the RFC, and in March 1918 he became a temporary and unpaid lieutenant colonel in the new Air Ministry's Directorate of Manning to work as Controller of the Women's Royal Air Force.*

Variously described as 'small but intimate' and 'possessed of atmosphere and charm', the new Club had 22 bedrooms and, according to *The Times*, was furnished and fitted up in the most artistic and comfortable way, with one of the best smoking rooms in London. Its principal purpose, as described by Bersey, was to provide rooms for officers on sick leave in London, but as time went on its role expanded. In particular, as influential airmen were arguing more and more for the creation of an air service separate from the Navy and Army, they found their views in conflict with the majority of members of the long-established service clubs to which they had hitherto belonged, and the RFC Club came to provide a valuable meeting point for those of like mind.

Its significance was well demonstrated by the presence on the Committee of several important personalities. The Chairman was Lieutenant General Sir David Henderson who, when representing the RFC on the Army Council, had become convinced of the need for an independent Air Ministry and a unified air service; in the view of the then Major General Hugh Trenchard, himself an important member of the RFC Club, it was Henderson – not he – to whom belonged the title 'Father of the Royal Air Force'. Other notable figures on the Committee included two more Major Generals, John Salmond and Sefton Brancker. Both were founder

* National Archives (formerly Public Record Office). WO 339/128280; *Women in Air Force Blue*, by Beryl Escott, pp 74–7.

members of the RFC who had commanded Wings in France and were now filling senior appointments in the Aeronautics Directorate of the War Office. Salmond would eventually succeed Trenchard as Chief of Air Staff and later become President of the RAF Club; Brancker, a subsequent Club Chairman, played a leading role in the post-war development of civil aviation and was killed when the airship R101 crashed at Beauvais in 1930.

The Committee itself comprised both elected and appointed members, the latter by virtue of their official positions in the RFC, and permanent membership of the Club was limited to gazetted RFC officers, of whom 75 per cent were required to be pilots and observers. Subscriptions were fixed at 3 guineas per annum. As indication of the modesty of the Club's operations, its monthly bank balance averaged some £400, and as a reminder of the straitened circumstances of the time the Committee Minute-Book recorded on 26 February 1918 that no meat was to be served for luncheon and members requiring meat for dinner must give previous notification.

By this time the RFC was about to come together with the Royal Naval Air Service to form the Royal Air Force, and a new title was obviously required. It was also clear that, as Brancker, now Chairman, put it, 'there were insuperable difficulties in carrying on the RFC Club (or its successor) in its present buildings'. As the RFC Club Committee started to address the problem, they found the ally they needed in the person of the first Viscount Cowdray.* The former Mr Weetman Pearson, now aged 62, had made his name and fortune abroad as a civil engineer, and in 1917, despite having never held public office, he was invited by the government to preside over the newly created Air Board, in order to oversee all design and production matters related to military aviation. This appointment brought him into close contact with Henderson, Brancker and their colleagues, and he not only directed a remarkable expansion of production but was quickly persuaded of the need to bring all military aviation together in a unified air service. Having then been made responsible for drafting the Bill setting up the new Air Ministry, he was widely expected, not least by Trenchard, to become the first Air Minister, but the Prime Minister, Lloyd George, had other ideas and Cowdray was cast aside. All he could now do for his airmen friends and the Royal Air Force he had helped create was to provide his practical support for the establishment of

---

* Spender, J. A. *Life of Weetman Pearson, 1st Vicount Cowdray*, p. 265; Anthony Le Jeune, in *The Gentlemen's Clubs of London*, Macdonald and Janes, 1979; Raleigh and Jones, *The War in the Air*, vol. 6 Chap. 20.

an RAF Club, which he offered to Brancker in a letter dated 30 October 1918. There was, too, a personal reason: his wish to commemorate one of his sons who had been killed serving as a despatch rider with the RFC early in the war. When Brancker immediately accepted Cowdray's offer of help on the 31st, his letter concluded:

> A more valuable form of assistance at this point in the history of the youngest of the Services could not have been conceived, and your name will go down to the coming generations of airmen, not only as their first Minister, but as their greatest personal benefactor.

Two days later came another tribute to Cowdray for his generosity, this time from the Air Council. As a raison d'être for the Club its terms are as valid today as they were then:

> The Council feel strongly that the establishment of such a club as Your Lordship contemplates will not only be a boon to the officers individually but that, apart from the social amenities and inter-course which it will offer, it will also contribute powerfully to securing full unity in spirit and in feeling in the now unified flying services of the Crown. In a sphere which is outside Government scope the club will, in a most happy and opportune manner, supplement what direct Government effort can provide and create for the officers of the Royal Air Force a social meeting place and an atmosphere which, though they could hardly proceed from state initiative, are none the less, in the Council's opinion, most valuable and indeed essential. The Club will thus serve a most important public service and will advance materially the fundamental realiz-ation of the policy over the inauguration of which Your Lordship, as President of the Air Board, presided.*

Cowdray's letter of 30 October had also contained a cheque for £100,000, sufficient to ensure a permanent Club House worthy of the airmen and of their 'brilliant and superlative heroic work', and he had gone on to invite his colleagues of the first Air Ministry to join him in finding a suitable building and preparing and equipping it as a Club. Initial suggestions

* National Archives: AIR 6640 (part of A2/71).

included Lord Salisbury's house in Arlington Street and the Stafford Hotel in St James's Place, but it was Cowdray himself who soon discovered that the home of the London Lyceum Club, a splendid house at No 128 Piccadilly, next door to the Cavalry Club (founded in 1890), was on the market. Established in 1904, the Lyceum had in its earlier days possessed up to 2,000 lady members, all 'working seriously at or having a sincere interest in literature, science, art or music', but at the end of the war financial problems were compelling it to move elsewhere; it still meets today.* The building had originally been constructed between 1887 and 1892 by Gillow and Company to house their new Piccadilly Club, but this did not last long and between 1903 and 1905 it was briefly used by the Imperial Service Club. The site itself had been occupied since the early eighteenth century by 'The Running Horse', one of a number of inns built in fields on the north side of Piccadilly at the time when the May Fair had become an annual West London event, providing the citizenry with 'music, shows, drinking, gambling, raffling, lotteries, stage plays and drolls'. The inns also came to serve the local drovers and horsemen (among them the Tattersalls). The Running Horse was described too as a house frequented by soldiers, and the Freemasons' Grenadier Lodge met there in the 1740s. Eventually, in 1872, it was acquired by Needs and Company, a firm of lockmakers, and fifteen years later the site was disposed of for redevelopment. Several eighteenth-century pewter tankards inscribed 'The Running Horse' were recovered in 1920 and are still displayed in the Club.

In selecting 128 Piccadilly for the Club, Cowdray was influenced by its proximity to No 6 Park Lane, hitherto used for carriage stables, horse stables and livery yards. This would provide the space needed to extend the main building, and Cowdray duly acquired the ground leases for both properties. Then, concerned to ensure that the Club should be properly conducted as befitting officers of the RAF, he transferred the leases and all the property to a small company, The Royal Air Force Club Company Limited, which would act as a Trust Company with £1,000 capital and license the Club itself to use the premises. Cowdray also stipulated that, after 21 years, provided the Club had carried out its obligations satisfactorily, it would have the right to purchase all the shares of the Company at par.

Meanwhile, with much work to be done before 128 Piccadilly could be brought into use, the new RAF Club needed a temporary home, and

* Smedley, C. 'The Founding of the London Lyceum Club in 1904'.

the Provisional Committee which had been set up under the chairmanship of General Oliver Swann* decided to seek the tenancy of 13 Bruton
Street from Lieutenant Colonel Bersey. So, with the backing of Lord
Cowdray, who agreed the immediate expenditure of £5,000 from his
initial gift, it was arranged on 19 December 1918 for the new RAF Club
to open at Bruton Street on 1 January 1919, with all members of the RFC
Club becoming ipso facto members. Three years were now to elapse –
rather than the one year first estimated – before the new building could
be made ready, and by then some of the questions that were to affect the
Club in the long term had already been addressed. The most important of
these concerned the long-term costs of running the Club, and the most
critical aspect – one which has continued ever since to challenge the
management – was the balance to be struck between membership
numbers and the level of subscriptions. When the Finance Sub-
Committee first considered this in December 1920 the membership stood
at 1,780, and this would need to be trebled if the current 5–7 guineas
annual subscription was to be maintained. The Committee was far from
optimistic. The officer corps now numbered less than 3,000 and was
unlikely to grow significantly; the many younger men were not highly
paid, and membership was certainly beyond the means of those who
were married. Moreover, when Sir Sefton Brancker suggested that the
Royal Aero Club,† now seeking bigger premises, be invited to amalga-
mate, his proposal was rejected as contrary to the spirit of Lord
Cowdray's gift; it was hoped that those of its members who were eligible
might wish to join the RAF Club in their own right. Cowdray himself,
however, thought the Sub-Committee unnecessarily apprehensive. In its
new premises he was confident that it would earn new trading income,
particularly from bedroom lettings, and would gain more members both
from serving officers and from the 30,000 or so who had held wartime
commissions. In any case, he told them, 'he was behind them' – a
statement which Brigadier General More, the Committee Chairman and

* A distinguished naval aviator, Swann had played a major role in developing the wartime
RNAS. He retired from the RAF in 1929, having been Air Member for Personnel (AMP) and
then CinC Middle East.

† The Royal Aero Club was founded in 1901 as a Club for balloonists. Its principal role is
to coordinate, promote and protect all forms of recreational and competitive air sport in
the UK and to represent UK air sport internationally. Since 1908 it has made awards to
recognise achievement in aviation.

at that time Director of Personal Services in the Air Ministry, interpreted as a promise to give further financial help if necessary.

At the same time, there were various Committee debates about 'conduct unbecoming'; for the Club to establish a reputable status in London and to represent the Royal Air Force in a proper light, it was important for criticisms and complaints to be firmly dealt with in the early days. Bouncing cheques were one problem; in July 1920 no fewer than ten such cheques were outstanding, but after several meetings the Committee decided against proceeding to the County Court as such action would be derogatory to the prestige of the Club and the Royal Air Force. 'Action would therefore be adjudicated on the original merits of each case, and drastic action ... would be brought to fruition only by gradual steps of increasing severity', read the Minutes. Several members offered as excuse their fathers' failures to pay their monthly allowances. Public misconduct was another problem. When in September 1920, for example, the resignation of one Captain Henley was demanded, action was impossible, decided the Committee, 'since first-hand evidence was unobtainable from the managers or chuckers-out of the theatres and music halls concerned who were compelled in their own interests to say that their houses of entertainment were orderly'. Drunkenness, one of his offences, was considered at several Committee meetings to be having a serious effect on the tone of the Club and may not have been unconnected with 'the bad habit of sleeping in the Reading Room or Lounge after the Club closed'. Maybe the Club management itself was not blameless; in April 1919, having been offered whisky by the gallon, they purchased fifty gallons. Some Club members were undoubtedly continuing the 'hard drinking, hard flying' ethos of the RFC, and in autumn 1920 the House Committee withdrew its demand for an Emergency General Meeting to consider disorderly conduct only when the General Committee promised to deal with it severely from now on.

There were, of course, more positive ways of starting to establish the status and reputation of the Club. One important issue was resolved very early on after the Air Council had refused to allow the Club to use the RAF Crest for its own purposes. The Club then submitted its own design, the Air Ministry counselled against using the Crown, and the Club appealed to the Lord Chamberlain who, with the College of Arms, raised no objection. As a result, after a six-months' battle, in June 1920 the Club Crest was approved on the lines of the RAF Crest, with the wording altered from 'Per Ardua ad Astra' to 'Royal Air Force Club'. Soon after this the Club acquired its first memorabilia, following on a Committee decision in August 1920 to collect war trophies, silver plate, squadron relics, records and photographs, together with complete editions of *Flight* and *Aeroplane*, and in due course to display such items around the walls of 128 Piccadilly. Among early donations received were a specimen case of hand-grenades and a set of 20 heads and masks of Asian and Sudanese game trophies. Portraits were less welcome. Whereas the gift of a painting of Air Commodore H. R. M. Brooke-Popham was accepted, a proposal to buy for 7½ guineas signed photogravure portraits of Earl Haig, Lord Beattie and Sir Hugh Trenchard was rejected in 1920 on the grounds that portraits or busts of famous men should not be displayed in the Club during their lifetime. Two years later the suggested purchase of an oil painting of Trenchard was again turned down.

A further means of enhancing the Club's prestige was the granting of honorary membership. The committee was empowered to elect for life Princes of the Blood Royal, Distinguished Officers of all three Services, and 'persons who have rendered signal service to the Royal Air Force, Royal Naval Air Service, Royal Flying Corps or the Royal Air Force Club'.* The military and political Heads of the Armed Services were also eligible for election for their terms of office. Moreover a category of Honorary Visitor enabled the net of distinction to be spread more widely, encompassing Foreign Ambassadors, Service Attachés and Distinguished Representatives of the Overseas Territories of the Empire when visiting the United Kingdom.

Other ways of establishing the external image of the Club were also found. On 26 June 1919, for example, a telegram was sent to Captain Alcock congratulating him and Lieutenant Whitten-Browne on completing the first non-stop trans-Atlantic flight in the Vickers Vimy: 'X-d good show. Vimy – Vidi – Vici – RAF Club'. Soon afterwards, in November, the RAF Club of New York, founded by Americans who had served in the RAF during the war, extended their hospitality to members of the RAF Club. In 1921 it was agreed that the Club would provide for entertaining members at the Hendon Pageant and at Lords for the Oxford-Cambridge Match – but not at Epsom or Ascot. Not all ideas, however, were accepted. In March 1920, a proposal

* In July 1930 the Committee was lamentably ignorant of its own rules when rejecting a request that Sir Frederick Royce (co-founder of Rolls-Royce) be elected an Honorary Life Member for services rendered to the RAF, on the grounds that Honorary Life Membership was granted for services rendered to the Club.

to make Sir Walter Raleigh (who had started writing the official Air Force History) an honorary member was unimaginatively turned down; then in August 1921, when Sir Sefton Brancker suggested that the Club should enter the Croydon Air Race against the Royal Aero Club, the Committee refused because it was inadvisable and 'derogatory for a Service Club to enter a race at a meeting which in character is commercial aviation'.

During these early years at Bruton Street the primary task of the House Committee was to plan and oversee the development of the Club's new building. They did so in association with Lord Cowdray, the architects whom he had appointed (Sir Aston Webb and Sons), and the building contractors, Messrs Trollope and Colls. The essential features proposed in 1919 consisted of two dining rooms with a combined seating capacity of some 200, a smoking room, a reading room and library, and 50 members' bedrooms (with 35 more for staff). Ladies, who were to have their own entrance into the Club from Old Park Lane, would have their own smoking and drawing room on the second floor and be allowed into one of the dining rooms. Additional facilities would include squash courts, a swimming bath (convertible to a concert hall if necessary), billiard tables, garage space (with one or two cars for hire to members), a laundry, hairdressing and telephones. By 1921, the busiest year in the programme for building, decorating, furnishing, equipping and staffing, the swimming pool and garage had been written out and the number of members' bedrooms increased to 63. Of these 15 were to be set aside for 'long occupation' of up to six months with the possibility of extension. In fact, when building work had been completed the Club opened with 69 bedrooms for members.

Meanwhile, in the autumn of 1920 General More had been obliged to discuss the escalating costs with Lord Cowdray. The benefactor had always recognised that these would substantially exceed his initial donation, and in April 1920 had raised his offer to £220,000. Now, thanks to a huge rise in the cost of materials and labour, these were estimated at £350,000, and Cowdray, reluctant to go that far, again increased his donation to £250,000 and told Sir Aston Webb to ensure that the final figure would not exceed £310,000. In the event it ended up at the £350,000 previously estimated.

By the end of the year other pressures were building up, notably the unsuitability of 13 Bruton Street for the growing amount of business the Club urgently needed to attract, and difficulties over its lease. In December the Committee therefore suggested that 128 Piccadilly be partially opened in May 1921 in time to cater for the London Season, but the architects refused, knowing that Lord Cowdray would prefer to wait until the new Club was complete. The Committee returned to the attack in February 1921, again urging the significance of the coming season's business, and in March they discussed the implications of the imminent acquisition of the Bruton Street lease by Almack's Club. In June, however, when notice was received that Bruton Street's club licence would shortly be withdrawn, Almack's had to back out and the RAF Club was able to extend its lease until January 1922.

So the Club made the best it could of the 1921 season at Bruton Street, whose doors were finally closed on 17 December. Then, after being permitted to use the Stratford Club over Christmas, members were allowed into 128 Piccadilly on 2 January 1922. It had originally been hoped that King George V would consent to open the Club formally, but the request was turned down on the grounds that he had recently refused to open the new Guards Club: he and Queen Mary would like, however, to inspect the building afterwards. On the understanding that the opening ceremony should be of as simple a character as possible, and that there would be no press representation, it was the Duke of York who subsequently agreed to do the honours.

In anticipation of the great day, the Club held a special dinner on 15 February 1922 to honour Lord Cowdray, whose generosity had made it all possible and who was already its first President. Then, on 24 February, the Duke of York, later King George VI, arrived to open the Club's new home, which was formally presented by Lord Cowdray to the Club's first trustees, Rear-Admiral Sir Godfrey Paine,* Sir David Henderson and Sir John Baird.[†] With it came the lease, which was granted to the Trustees on 2 September 1920 and ran for 99 years from 24 June 1920. The celebrations were completed on 14 March, when King George V and Queen Mary paid their promised visit;[‡] the photograph of this event hangs above the Visitors' Book in the Lobby, but when the silver pen they used came up for auction in Gloucestershire 76 years later, the Club was unfortunately outbid.

* Paine, Commandant of the Central Flying School 1912–15 and last Director of the RNAS, was Inspector General, RAF, in 1919.

† Baird, later Viscount Stonehaven, was Permanent Under-Secretary of State in the Air Ministry during 1918.

‡ Articles in *Flight* dated 5 January and 2 March 1922 (courtesy of the Royal Aeronautical Society).

CHAPTER 2

MONEY AND MEMBERSHIP

The understandable euphoria engendered in the Club by these opening ceremonies was not to be long-lived, and on the critical issue it still faced, namely membership, there were many doubts. Lord Cowdray himself, as we have seen (p. 15), remained confident about the future prospects but few who were in the know really shared his high hopes at that time.

The numbers game tells its own story. In 1921, when the immense exodus of wartime personnel was complete, the entire RAF officer strength had fallen by 90 per cent, and of the survivors only 631 (i.e., fewer than 25 per cent) were members of the Club; retired officers brought the total membership to a mere 1,650. From then until 1939, when the total reached 2,138, the membership never exceeded 2,101 (in 1928), and it averaged substantially less. Of these the serving officers rarely comprised more than one-third. So not only did membership fail to reach the substantial numbers clearly expected by Cowdray, it did not even achieve the more modest target of 2,300 set in 1932.

Given the circumstances of the inter-war years, such disappointing figures are not really surprising. For one thing, in the 1920s the RAF itself was under almost unrelenting pressure from the other two Services, each determined to regain control of its own air service in order to strengthen its position in the fight for scarce national resources. There was little love lost between them and the young upstart which was pressing its case for the full exploitation of air power. For a long while there was no certainty which way the battle would go, and some of the RAF's more senior officers, who were long-standing members of their old naval and military clubs, preferred to remain in their familiar surroundings. Indeed, as Sir Maurice Dean later wrote in *The RAF and Two World Wars*, some military clubs had actually barred RAF officers in 1919: 'social ostracism was the order of the day'. Some younger officers, too, were influenced by what they perceived as the RAF's uncertain future.

Later on, of course, this factor ceased to apply but others grew in importance, and not least the nature of the officer corps. Among Trenchard's well-conceived recruitment schemes were the five-year short service commissions, the auxiliary squadrons and the university air squadrons, all aimed at appealing to young men who – at least initially – only wanted to fly and probably just for a few years. They came from wide social and educational backgrounds and were rarely conversant with the atmosphere and traditions of London clubs or indeed prepared to subscribe to one of them out of their meagre pay. The Cranwell cadets who were to provide Trenchard's permanent cadre also had more varied origins than their Army and Navy opposite numbers and tended to be less 'clubbable'. Air Chief Marshal Sir David Lee (see p. 84) remembers being encouraged to join the Club when he graduated in 1932, but for him and most of his colleagues it had little appeal. He felt he could find better ways of spending his small salary and since he was about to be posted overseas could see no point; not until nearly 30 years later, as an Air Vice-Marshal, did he sign up.

Lee's experience was typical of most young officers in those days. Throughout the 1920s and early 1930s the great majority of the RAF's operational squadrons were located overseas, particularly in India, the Middle East and Egypt, so it was there that the newly qualified aviators were usually sent. Even the minority who knew of the Club's existence saw it as an irrelevance and throughout these years there was little injection of new blood into the Club's serving membership. In the later 1930s, on the other hand, attitudes began to change. The progressive expansion of the RAF in face of the growing threat from Germany not only brought in many more recruits but also led to the creation of new fighter and bomber squadrons for service in the home country, where there was more incentive to join the Club. Air Chief Marshal Sir Lewis Hodges, who graduated from Cranwell in 1936, is another who remembers being urged to enrol and, in the context of a currently expanding air force with a challenging situation to meet, he opted to do so. The fact remained that many of the RAF's new home bases were in areas relatively remote from London and the overall growth of member-ship among the younger officers remained right up to the outbreak of war disappointingly small. Indeed, as a proportion of the rapidly growing officer corps the Club's serving membership was steadily declining. To a considerable extent, therefore, this failure to attract worthwhile numbers of new recruits in the 1920s and 1930s was due to circumstances outside the Club's own control. It must now be asked how the Committee handled its affairs at this time and whether it could have done better.

For the first few years the Club remained under the wise guidance of Lord Cowdray, who on his death in 1927 was succeeded as President by his son and subsequently in 1936 by his grandson. There was continuity too in the chairmanship (see Appendix A). Brigadier General More, who had overseen the Committee since 1921, held the post until 1929, and his successor, Air Commodore McNeece Foster (who would make a name for himself in influential staff appointments during the Second World War), served for the next seven years. Then, in 1937, after a brief interlude for Air Marshal Sir Frederick 'Ginger' Bowhill (soon to become CinC Coastal Command), Colonel Bersey, who had stayed as a key member of the Committee, returned to the chair and remained there until the end of the war. There were also only four Secretaries between 1920 and 1941; three were long-term: Major R. D. Anderson, Group Captain A. B. Burdett and Wing Commander C. P. Ogden.* The General Committee itself, responsible for the management, conduct and direction of the Club and its premises, had 24 members, all elected at the Annual General Meeting (AGM) each March. They met monthly, and the seven who comprised the Executive Committee met fortnightly.

They and their colleagues had much to do, and for much of the time they faced a difficult hand-to-mouth existence. In October 1922 a first-year loss of £12,412 was reported (no small sum in those days) and while inevitably this led to a discussion on the practicalities of increasing the membership, the immediate financial situation needed urgent attention. Fortunately the Club's bankers, Williams Deacons, had already indicated their willingness to help, and it was agreed to seek an overdraft. Should the debt persist, the Committee decided that it would accept an offer which it thought Lord Cowdray had made, namely to support the issue of debentures up to £30,000. At a Special Club Meeting a year later General More had to report that it was time to face the fact that the Club's debt was likely to prove permanent; a second overdraft must therefore be sought, and the issue of debentures must be arranged with Lord Cowdray. Unfortunately More then discovered that since no written covenant existed to that effect, the debenture scheme was impracticable, but, with the financial situation worsening, he met the bank manager and reported on his helpful attitude. Essentially the bank was willing to help the Club

---

* Anderson had served in the Boer and First World Wars. Burdett, who had flown with the RFC in France, retired in 1930 after serving in the Air Ministry and as AOC 21 Group; Ogden, also ex-RFC, had later worked in the Stores and Accounts Branch.

in every way possible over the financial difficulties which were bound to occur in its early years; a £5,000 overdraft was therefore negotiated, guaranteed on future subscriptions rather than debentures. The Club had indeed been fortunate in its bank manager.

Meanwhile, in October 1923 Bersey had reported on ways of reducing the trading deficit and paying for future redecorations and renovations. Nothing very constructive emerged. Neither expenditure nor wages could be reduced; indeed comparison of the pay scales with those of other Service clubs showed those of the RAF Club to be considerably lower. Even so, he went on, staff increments were not being paid this year; nevertheless, since general wages and prices were falling and the Club was holding its rates steady, this effectively constituted a pay rise!

During these initial years the Committee worked hard to address the membership situation, having first formalised its rules for eligibility. The essential qualification was that members must hold or have held the King's Commission in the RAF, RNAS or RFC, or in certain specified associated forces. For subscription purposes there were three categories. Town Members paid the full rate, i.e., 10 guineas per annum. Country Members, namely those domiciled outside a 50-mile radius measured as the crow would fly from Charing Cross, paid 7 guineas, provided that they did not reside in London for more than 60 days a year. 'Foreign' Members, i.e., that significant proportion of serving officers who were stationed overseas, were required to pay only 2 guineas. While the Committee was empowered to vary these rates, they in fact remained unchanged until January 1949.

The first measures designed to increase the membership were taken in 1922, when Halton, Cranwell and each of the three overseas Commands (Egypt, Iraq and India) were invited to nominate liaison officers to act as ex-officio members of the Committee and encourage their officers to join the Club. Letters were also sent individually to senior serving officers who were not members, and 24-hours' free use of the Club was offered as bait; this particular privilege was rapidly withdrawn after some 'regrettable cases'! Such measures achieved little success, and neither did the special Membership Committee set up in 1925. One of its proposals, to issue an illustrated booklet to advertise the Club, was rejected because 'it might give rise to hostile criticism'. Nor did a suggestion from the Editor of the RAF Diary to include details of the Club meet with approval: 'the Club had a policy of non-advertising'.

By now the annual trading loss was being steadily converted to a marginal profit, a tribute to careful management, but the Club's overall financial situation remained serious and in 1926 the Committee decided to seek a mortgage on its premises with the Prudential. This was eventually agreed to a maximum of £30,000 for 23 years; half would be paid as soon as arranged, and the rest could be called as required. As More explained to an Extraordinary General Meeting on 26 June 1928, the mortgage was being sought because it was not good to be living from hand to mouth by borrowing against the following year's subscriptions. The money would pay off the earlier revenue deficits and cover planned major improvements. It was approved unanimously.

When General More relinquished the Chair in 1929, he and his Committee had done their best to put the Club on a sound footing and could hardly have expected the calamitous effects of the Wall Street Crash and the world-wide financial depression that ensued. For the RAF the next few years were to be particularly difficult, with further build-up almost impossible and searching questions being asked about the whole future of military aviation, particularly its bombing role. The Club records contain little detail about the impact of these problems on its viability, though a report in October 1929 which showed expenditure increasing and the general financial state deteriorating coincided with a practical instruction issued by the Secretary. This stated that restaurant carvers were to serve smaller portions, that omelettes were to contain one and a half rather than two eggs, and that bags belonging to members of staff were to be searched before they left the Club.

In May 1930 the financial climate had led to a fall in restaurant, bar and bedroom receipts, and in October the Executive Committee went so far as to recommend suspending the entrance fee in order to encourage new members, a suggestion which the General Committee rejected. In February 1932, however, the 1931 balance sheet was considered very satisfactory 'in view of the unprecedented financial depression throughout the year'. Even so, four months later, the Committee was expressing concern about declining credit balances as a consequence of the 'prevailing adverse conditions', and referring to 'a classic pincer': without the intended development programme on which the Committee had been working the Club would not reach its minimum membership target, yet without such numbers it could not prudently implement its programme. The Committee's decision in July 1932 was inevitable: the

24

programme must be deferred. Then in November the Committee bit the bullet and waived the entrance fee, bringing in 100 new applications in just over a month. Shortly before this the Committee had renewed its earlier appeals to RAF units, in particular the flying training schools, and on 28 April 1931 it was reported that 23 of the 24 members recently elected were from just one of these, RAF Digby. Four years later Cranwell was similarly praised when a list of 34 new members included 26 of its newly qualified graduates. Such achievements were, however, few and far between, and the overall membership level remained stuck just below 2,000 for several more years. So for a while the Club continued along an indeterminate path, unable to tackle the underlying weaknesses and regularly describing its financial situation as satisfactory, but in reality relying on the Bank overdraft to meet its bills. In 1933, a typical year, the Committee applied in March for the 'usual half-yearly overdraft' of £2,000 to be secured against July's half-yearly subscription income; in July the next overdraft of £2,500 was to be secured against January 1934's subscriptions. Occasionally there was a warning, as in August 1934 when the Auditor stated that the decreasing profits were due to members spending less in the Club, 'the general experience at the present time', but not until 1935 did it seem that the scene was about to change. This was the year when Stanley Baldwin's General Election victory provided the impetus for speeding up the RAF's expansion programme in face of the growing threat from Hitler's Luftwaffe, and it seemed to the Club that its long-awaited improvement scheme could no longer be delayed.

Colonel Bersey, still the Committee's éminence grise, accordingly submitted a comprehensive report on 27 October. This analysed the membership, the Club's accommodation, the staff and the various costings, and went on to propose a whole series of physical improvements. These, he predicted, would bring in a large number of new members each of whose spending would produce an average annual income to the Club of £15.10s. 0d. Strongly endorsing this programme, the Executive Committee observed that the 1,000 increase in the RAF's officer corps that was now in prospect would yield another 256 Club members – or more, since the increase would be for home defence. Yet, for all the optimism generated by this report, translating it into reality was an entirely different matter. The years 1936 and 1937 were marked, not by the hoped-for growth in revenue but by continuing decline, variously attributed to lower bedroom lettings, sales of food and liquor, and usage of the squash courts. Nor did increased rates and taxes help the situation.

It was under these depressing circumstances that in 1937 Sir Frederick Bowhill had to relinquish the Chair after just one year. At the AGM on 1 July another senior and influential member, Air Commodore (later MRAF) Sholto Douglas, commented perceptively that, given the difficult times the Club was going through, both financially and otherwise, a Chairman should be appointed who would be able to devote the necessary time to the Club; Douglas therefore proposed Colonel Bersey, 'who was really the founder of the Club and knew more than anyone else'. His proposal was accepted, and the rationale made sense. Bowhill had done all he could, not least in urging members to devote time to persuading others to join, but he and other very senior officers at that time were too heavily committed to their RAF duties to give the Club the attention it needed. Whether Bersey was the right man to take it on was another matter. Now aged 62, he had certainly served the Club well but as a key committee member he seems never to have been particularly critical or forward-thinking. Arguably, however, what the Club was most in need of as the war clouds gathered was a safe pair of hands, and these were what Bersey provided over the next eight years.

Hardly had Bersey taken over than the Secretary counselled caution about the financial prospects, reminding the Committee that the RAF's current expansion meant that large numbers of officers previously stationed near London were now being posted to new aerodromes in distant parts of the country, from where they were less likely either to join the Club or use its facilities. The Chairman, however, retained his customary confidence. In October, for example, he referred to the recent nine-month deficit of £921 and predicted that recent administrative changes would lead to rapid improvement. Then in February 1938 at the AGM, introducing a new balance sheet showing a £1,502 deficit, he explained the need to increase the annual income by £1,200 so as to compensate for increased staff wages, reduced bedroom rentals and subscription income, and loss of profit from the recently abandoned Hendon Air Display. Since no savings could be made without seriously damaging Club amenities, the main effort must be devoted to acquiring more members, and to that end a new brochure had already been distributed to RAF stations. The election of 90 new members since 1 January

1938 was a good augury, he concluded. Nevertheless, in April the Committee was still discussing such realities as a continuing decline in room rentals, a reduced number of permanent residents (17 per month in 1936; eight in 1938), the growing pressure of work on RAF officers and the continuing transfers of members away from London. By March 1939, however, when the Club held its last AGM before the outbreak of war, Bersey again felt able to be 'up-beat'. The debit balance of the previous year was down by two-thirds, bedroom lettings had risen a little, catering was very satisfactory, with 60,000 meals having been served in 1938, staff wages and costs were only slightly up, and the overall profit on trading operations in 1935-8 was £8,000. 'Special expenses' over the same period had come to £11,000. Membership, he concluded, now stood at 2,141, a net increase of 133 over the previous year, and the way forward was to expand it further. Thus the final pre-war months did witness some slight improvement in the Club's situation and under all the circumstances not much more could realistically have been achieved.

What the Club had signally failed to do in the inter-war years, however, was to develop and extend its various facilities, though this was certainly not due to any lack of ideas. As early as 1925, for example, a 'highly attractive scheme' was considered to convert the Ballroom to a ladies' dining room, the small dining room to a writing room, and the Mezzanine Suite to a reading room; the necessary expenditure, however, was thought unjustifiable until the membership reached 2,250. In 1928 another Ballroom alteration coupled with the building of three new bedrooms was discussed and similarly rejected. A considerably more extensive scheme was mooted in 1930: this entailed selling the Park Lane Flats (described as an incubus, not an asset), moving the Members' Bar, enlarging the ground floor cloakrooms, constructing two new 'standard' squash courts and converting the existing ones to female staff accommo-dation, and building seven new bedrooms. While most of these proposals were firmly postponed 'in view of the general depression', an offer of £2,650 for the Flats was accepted in September 1931; in consequence ten members' bedrooms had to be allocated to the 24 displaced female staff, and at the same time the Steward's office in the basement was converted to accommodate eight employees. Fairly soon afterwards the Bar was moved and the cloakrooms enlarged, but nothing extensive was consid-ered until 1935, when Colonel Bersey produced his major report on the future development of the Club (p. 25).

This report envisaged extending the existing lounge and bar area on the ground floor into a much larger lounge and constructing a new bar and two separate billiard rooms. On the first floor would be a new and larger library releasing the Mezzanine Suite for private functions, and on the higher floors would be more bedrooms, new staff dormitories and two 'standard' squash courts. The full scheme would cost £23,000, nearly all of which could be met by calling on the remaining balance of the original Prudential loan. The Committee, confident that extra business generated by new members would generate the necessary additional income, initially accepted these proposals with enthusiasm. At a special meeting shortly afterwards, however, it was a different story as the Club Auditor strongly counselled caution. The new members the Club was looking for, he said, would be largely junior officers who as a body would not be good recruiting material for the Club and were unlikely to bring much spending power. Moreover, the expenses of such projects usually escalated, and in any case building costs were expected soon to increase greatly. Crucially, he concluded, by calling on the £30,000 total loan from the Prudential the Club would exhaust its borrowing power. There was no answer to this, and despite a final abortive attempt in 1937 to push through the new squash courts, that was the end of the last pre-war development scheme.

CHAPTER 3

CLUB LIFE AND ATMOSPHERE

R ight from the start it was appreciated that the Club would need to convey to its members and their friends some feel for the developing history and ethos of the young Air Force from which it had sprung. The various Naval and Army Clubs, some of them much older, were able to commemorate events, personalities and traditions which dated back over centuries, whereas the RAF Club was having to start from scratch in an entirely novel situation. Indeed, it may well have seemed to its leading figures that it had little chance of ever achieving comparison with its competitors.

A start was nevertheless quickly made when in July 1922 the Committee decided to commission the war artist Sir William Orpen to paint a portrait of Lord Cowdray, the Club's benefactor and first President. Members were invited to subscribe a guinea each towards its cost and on 30 August 1923 it was unveiled in the presence of Lord and Lady Cowdray by Sir Samuel Hoare, Secretary-of-State for Air. It was then placed in the panel above the fireplace in the Smoking-Room, which was situated on the Ground Floor in what is now the Dining Room. In 1928 a painting of Flight Lieutenant Samuel Kinkead, who had been killed attempting to break the world speed record, was unveiled, this time by Sir Hugh Trenchard, but only a few months later the Club suffered a fit of obtuseness. Having received an offer from Rolls-Royce to present a portrait of Sir Arthur Whitten-Browne (Alcock's navigator – p.17) the Committee turned it down on the grounds that 'the Club does not hang pictures of living members'. This so-called 'policy' certainly did not apply in 1930 when it was unanimously agreed to commission a portrait of Trenchard himself; painted by Oswald Birley, this was paid for by members' subscription and delivered to the Club on 1 December 1930. Three years later Sir John Salmond also completed his term as CAS and was similarly honoured by the Club, his portrait being painted by Cuthbert Orde, particularly well-known later on for his wartime drawings of Fighter Command pilots. Both officers had strongly backed the Club in its formative years, Ever since, of the RAF's most senior officers, only Presidents have been commemorated in this way.

During these years the Club also acquired a miscellany of game trophies offered by members. According to the Committee Minutes a pair of elephant tusks came first, followed by an elephant's foot (thought suitable for conversion to a ground ashtray when funds permitted), two panther skins, a rhino horn, four hippo's teeth, a lion's head and a tiger's head. In 1931 an estimate of 10 guineas was accepted for 'inspecting, disinfecting and touching them up'. There seems to have been limited enthusiasm for aviation artefacts. In 1924 two propellers, three machine-guns, two joysticks and a portion of Zeppelin propeller and clock were refused. Some items, however, were accepted, including a German shell case, an original model aeroplane made by Santos-Dumont in 1900, and a pound note flown across the Atlantic by Alcock and Browne.

Much more significant and appropriate was the decision on 7 January 1937 to collect copies of squadron badges; up to 200 would be needed and they would not be cheap if quality were to be maintained. Enquiries were therefore made of the Chester Herald,* who agreed to certify full-scale copies of the originals for members to present to the Club at 4 guineas each plus the cost of the frame. The Committee decided to go ahead, letting members know that only these certified copies would be accepted for display. Thus began a scheme which continues to this day and has given the Club one of its most evocative and historically important features, the Badge Corridor in which altogether 357 badges of RAF squadrons and other RAF units are now permanently on show.

Unfortunately the Club archives contain no floor plans or photographs to indicate the internal layout of the building between the wars. A detailed inventory of fixtures, fittings and furnishings compiled in 1924 has, however, survived and this forms the basis for the description of the amenities given in Appendix B. The changes in use of the Club's public rooms, insofar as these can be ascertained from the records, are given in Appendix C.

The need to improve the quality and quantity of the residential accommodation was certainly well appreciated in the early days, but little could be done in practice and the 60 or so bedrooms available for letting to

---

* The use of squadron badges dates back to the RFC. Some years after the formation of the RAF it was decided that the adoption and use of badges should be properly controlled, and in 1936 the office of Inspector of RAF Badges was created. In view of the connection with traditional heraldry, the Chester Herald was appointed as the first holder of this post. Since then any unit wishing to have a badge has arrived at its design in consultation with the Inspector – nowadays the Garter King of Arms.

members – rarely en suite – were generally accepted as adequate; few complaints are recorded. The hire charges varied according to position, size and convenience, and some members were sufficiently satisfied to take advantage of the bye-law permitting them to reside for up to a year. The rules also stipulated that strangers were not allowed into the Club without the Secretary's express permission, and there was specific reference to members' manservants. They might enter only their master's bedroom and bathroom, were not to receive any accommodation or refreshment in the Club, and could remain on the premises only for the time necessary to perform their duties.

The nature and quality of the catering facilities attracted rather more attention. An early problem arose in 1923, when the Committee agreed urgent action to destroy the beetles which were increasing at an alarming rate in the Servery, Still Room, American Bar and Basement. In 1926, after two members had been served with 'tainted fish and cold meats', the Secretary was instructed to obtain estimates for the installation of suitable cold storage. Two years later complaints at a special meeting led to the creation of a sub-committee to investigate the food and service in the Dining Room, and in 1929 it was decided that the Club should not supply foreign meat – though no reason was stated. Meanwhile the conversion of the Small Dining Room into a quick lunch bar was proving popular, not least perhaps because smoking was allowed. While the Club policy was in general permissive, smoking had so far been banned in the dining areas to the annoyance of senior members such as Sefton Brancker, and to them the lunch bar came as a welcome breakthrough. The issue never went away. In 1933, for example, smoking in the Dining Room was again rejected, partly because members would linger at table, thereby keeping the staff late, and also since a smoke-laden atmosphere would be unacceptable to many members. The quick lunch room itself seems to have become a permanent feature to the extent that, such were the numbers now using it, in 1938 part of the first-floor corridor was screened off as an overflow.

The main Dining Room did not suffer from the competition, though the introduction of a 'house dinner' (1927), a set lunch (1930) and a 'club dinner' (1933) suggests that the management recognised the need to adapt. Not always, however, did things run smoothly. In 1932, the Secretary was instructed to interview the Head Waiter and his Assistant 'because of poor supervision in the Dining Room'; in 1934 a complaints book was instituted; and in 1936 the Executive Committee resolved that in view of the room's very unattractive atmosphere and the poor standard of its service, a more effective Steward must be appointed. Such situations were nothing new: way back in 1922 the Chef had been dismissed for 'insobriety, inattention to detail and lack of control', and a head waitress was dismissed as having 'no authority, no sense of responsibility and no sense of her duties'. At the same time abnormally large breakages of glass and crockery led the Committee to consider a levy on staff wages in order to pay for losses and encourage greater care – an idea which was rapidly discarded as likely to cause discontent. In 1923 the Dining Room Steward had been removed for 'inaccuracy, inability to get on with the staff, lack of gumption and initiative'; in 1925 his successor was given notice for incompetence; in 1929 another Steward was 'too old and incapable', and in 1930 a Chef was dismissed for unsatisfactory accounting.

There were problems of other kinds too in the early days. One of these emerged in November 1922, when the Committee heard that Lady Cowdray – who was advising on refurnishing the Ballroom for use by the ladies as a tea and coffee lounge – intended to use it for regular 'thés dansants'. The immediate reaction was critical. These dances would be 'a somewhat novel departure for a Service Club', indeed they could cost the Club many members 'and the Service interest'. The Chairman, aware of the sensitivities, concluded that it would be unwise to embark on dances of this nature for the time being. He held an open mind, however, with regard to future developments which would doubtless be guided by public opinion and the trend of modern life in London. Fortnightly evening dances were in fact already in the programme, but not proving profitable because of the city's many counter-attractions, and in November 1923 they were discontinued. Ten years later, however, the Committee agreed to hold a New Year's Dinner and Dance; this set the scene for a successful annual event which continued until the war.

Special events too had their place in the Club calendar. The purely RAF ones seem to have gone unrecorded other than an Independent Air Force Dinner on 19 June 1922, but national celebrations were often marked, with the Club taking advantage of its position on the Processional Route for some of the Royal occasions. The first such event was on 8 February 1922 when members and guests viewed Princess Mary's Wedding Procession and lunched afterwards. A year later similar provision was made for the Duke of York's Wedding – but this time the Chef failed to prepare lunch for the expected 150 and was summarily dismissed. The RAF team's victories in the Schneider Trophy in 1927 and 1929 were next celebrated with a luncheon attended by the Air Minister and the Chief of Air Staff; the final outright victory in 1931 was marked by a full-scale dinner in the presence of the Duke of York.* The same year saw a General Election Night dinner and dance, with results projected on screens in the Ballroom and Members' Dining Room, and for the 1935 Election a supper was laid on accompanied by an improved results service. Shortly before this, elaborate arrangements had been made for viewing the Silver Jubilee Procession, and in November 1936 a Dinner Dance was held on Coronation Night.

The most regular pre-war event was the RAF's annual Hendon Air Display, where from 1922 until 1938 the Club Marquee, offering luncheon and tea, provided a most popular amenity. In 1927, for example, 750 lunches and 1,500 teas were available. On a sadder note, an active Committee member, Squadron Leader S. B. Collett, was killed while taking part in the Display on 30 June 1934. The Club's racing fraternity too were catered for, partly through sweepstakes for the Derby and Grand National (with the Club taking 10 per cent of the stakes for the Silver Fund), and partly by preparing picnic lunch hampers for use at race, river and motoring events. The Club had a firm rule about debts of honour: 'defaulters on the Turf' would lose their membership.

One particular sporting activity which was strongly backed in the early 1920s proved a failure. In May 1922, despite the Committee's initial misgivings on grounds of cost, it was decided to organise a Cricket Week at Eastbourne, and Air Commodore F. C. Halahan (Director of Aeronautical Inspection) agreed to oversee the venture. In September, Air Ministry anxieties about confusion between the RAF Club side and the RAF itself having been overcome, the Week went ahead. The Committee subsequently reported its great success: it had greatly raised the Club's prestige, the Prince of Wales, the MCC and the Mayor of Eastbourne had expressed appreciation, several new members had joined the Club, and the RAF Band had received many engagements as a direct result. On the other hand the Club had lost £200, which Halahan blamed on bad weather and lack of local support. In 1923 and 1924 the Week went to Hastings, but growing dissension among Club cricketers and influential players from the MCC, together with continuing financial losses, led to

* The Schneider Trophy now resides in the Science Museum.

several acrimonious meetings in the winter of 1924/5. Some cricketing members, including Halahan and Bersey, supported by Mr Percy Fender of the MCC, were keen to continue the Week, given the Mayor of Folkestone's offer to play host and the goodwill the event had created. Others criticised the contemporary national cricket scene, asserted that most Club members had little interest, and disapproved of the costs entailed. Eventually, in March 1925 the Club AGM ruled that the Cricket Week should cease unless there was a reasonable chance of recouping some of the earlier losses. Folkestone was duly cancelled and the saga ended with the write-off of the £660 loss incurred by the three previous events.

Golf on the other hand, though needing little Committee attention, was a success story from the start. On 21 February 1923 an invitation was accepted from the Bath Club to take part in an annual inter-club tournament and in December 1925 Major R. D. Anderson presented a Handicap Challenge Cup for this event. Two years later the RAF Club won the First Division and with one or two gaps has continued to compete ever since. Squash, too, has always been a Club activity, though controversial because of its accommodation requirements within the building itself. Two courts were provided, the services of a professional were obtained, and charges were initially fixed at a shilling per hour for members and two shillings for guests. Later, in 1931, members of the Cavalry Club were also allowed limited use. Unfortunately, however, the courts were less than standard size and by the 1930s, when Club members were eager to take full part in competition matches, there was much pressure to rebuild them. One proposal, seriously considered more than once, was to construct new ones on the Club roof, but legal problems, issues of neighbours' light, and above all lack of funds precluded any such scheme. So nothing was done and in 1938, when the Committee agreed that income from squash was reducing in all London Clubs thanks to increasing facilities elsewhere, they decided merely to replace the cement floors of the existing courts with wooden ones. Nevertheless the players continued to do themselves justice, to the extent of winning the 2nd Division Bath Cup in March 1939.

Another important attraction was the Billiard Room, whose two tables were located in what is today the Members' Bar. Rules for gentlemanly conduct were strictly laid down and they stipulated that the room was to be closed at 4 a.m.; only resident members were allowed in after the Club's closure at 1.30 a.m. On the whole the rules were obeyed, though in November 1927 the Committee had to instruct the Secretary to deal with complaints about 'general conduct and bad language'. Later, in 1935, the Committee rejected a proposal to accept an annual challenge for a Billiard Cup offered by the Constitutional Club, partly since the challenger was not a Service Club, and also since such matches, which would let non-members into the clubhouse, would not be popular with members. The Billiards Sub-Committee promptly resigned en bloc.

Card playing too was popular. A card room was provided from the start and here again strict regulations were laid down in the Club Rules. The permitted games of hazard were listed – Whist, Solo Whist, Bridge, Auction Bridge, Piquet, Ecarte, Bezique, Cribbage, Patience and Euchre – and the stakes for each game specified. Card debts of honour were to be settled within 48 hours and failure to do so without good cause would lead to 'removal from the list of members'. That there were problems here was shown in 1928, when the Executive Committee reported that non-permitted games were being played and went so far as to recommend that members of the Club should face annual re-election 'as there was a certain element that was not beneficial to its interest'. Understandably the Main Committee was unwilling to go this far, but instructed the Secretary to provide a monthly résumé of complaints.

The rules for these and other Club activities were specific on one subject that did not even cause significant controversy in those days. The squash courts were firmly closed to ladies, who initially were not even allowed to watch, a ban which was subsequently rescinded 'provided no refreshment of any sort was served to them'. The billiard and card rooms too were totally barred. In those days such restrictions were normal in gentlemen's clubs, reflecting the fact that ladies were generally given no membership status whatsoever, and some even refused them entry. The RAF Club's policy was to allow them to use the Club as guests. In the inter-war years, of course, there was no women's section of the RAF, so the Club had no need to consider whether and how female officers should be fitted into its structure. The ladies who used the Club were all civilians, either relatives or friends of men who were members.

It was, however, clear from the start that these ladies were determined to play their part in Club life, even though they had no formal status and were allowed to enter the building only through the side door at 6 Park Lane, where the notice at one time stated: 'Dogs, Luggage and Ladies'. That the Committee concerned itself with such matters is clear from the Minutes. On 1 March 1922 they decreed that the Ladies' Rooms were to close at 11 p.m.; soon afterwards they decided to close the Club to ladies on the night of the Independent Air Force Dinner, and at about the same time they first considered providing them with a separate dining area. Initially the ladies had used the west end of the Dining Room, but now it was proposed to adapt the Ballroom for them. A £2,000 estimate quickly ruled this idea out of court, whereupon it was decided to screen a section of the Dining Room for their use. The Ballroom conversion was considered again in 1924/5, still prompted by the objections of many members to the presence of ladies in their Dining Room. Air Vice-Marshal Brooke-Popham was one who strongly voiced the opinion that this was not only unpopular, but, particularly important, a brake on increased membership. The costings, however, remained prohibitive. Added to the capital expenditure there would be annual running costs almost as great, and the likely demand from the ladies would far from cover these.

Two further ladies' issues arose later. In 1928 the inadequacy of the Ladies' Waiting Room beside the Park Lane entrance was discussed by the Committee; stating that no better room was available, they observed that a member expecting a lady guest should be there to meet her, and that a lady calling on a member who was out 'naturally would not remain after being so informed'. Then in 1932, when it was agreed that an increase in ladies' accommodation would be very popular and produce substantial revenue, it was decided – despite the Chairman's 'total opposition' – to convert the library (today's Drawing Room) to a ladies' lounge and transfer the books to the Mezzanine Suite, a switch eventually accomplished in 1935. Waitresses also suffered from male prejudice. In 1929, for example, the Committee accepted that too many were employed in the Dining Room and that 'the appalling service' there was probably due to their lack of intelligence.

It was not only ladies' status that could cause concern. Between the wars it was taken for granted that His Majesty's officers would be of European descent, so when Pilot Officer K. Majumder, an Indian Officer who had just passed out from Cranwell, applied for membership in 1934 he presented the Committee with an awkward dilemma. Two of them protested emphatically against native officers of India being elected as either members or honorary visitors, but the others were conciliatory, agreeing to offer him Honorary Visitorship during the rest of his stay in England.

One more long-running subject of Committee discussion also needs further mention, i.e., 'conduct unbecoming' (see p. 16). Few meetings passed without having to deal with several incidents of bouncing cheques, and in 1927 Rule XXXVII was tightened up to read that when a cheque was returned the member should ipso facto be suspended and 'unless he can prove it was due to a mistake on the part of his bank ... or to circumstances outside his control ... he shall be called on to resign or be expelled'. In 1932, by which time the effects of the Depression were making the situation worse, the Committee considered the even more draconian measure of referring to the Air Ministry the names of serving officers who had defaulted and not paid up. Fortunately, on the advice of the Club Solicitor, this idea was not pursued. The circumstances of such incidents varied. In 1927, the father of an indebted flight lieutenant wrote to explain that he had failed to pay a promised remittance to his son's bank. In 1929 the Secretary, investigating a £15 default by one Captain Morley, was informed by his sister and wife that he had defrauded one and left the other; his resignation was accepted. In 1931 another officer tried to explain away a £50 debt 'because he was awaiting a legacy from his father's will'. In 1934 Flight Lieutenant Ward's second offence was treated leniently when it was stated on his behalf that he was suffering from the effects of an aeroplane crash the year before, and a year later he was again in trouble and added a family bereavement to his previous case. The Committee agreed sympathetically that the Chairman should interview him and 'obtain a promise concerning his future conduct'. In 1938, however, a firm line was taken with Wing Commander Brown, who was required to resign following his third offence.

The problem of drink-induced misbehaviour was inevitably an on-going concern for the Committee. Its significance was clearly recognised in March 1924 when Colonel Burleigh referred to the recent dismissal of a dissatisfied servant and outlined what might happen as a result. The Club could face a heavy fine, if not the loss of its licence, were this man to swear an affidavit before a JP which might lead to a warrant being issued to the police to enter the building after hours and discover what was going on. The Committee immediately agreed that the licensing laws must be strictly observed. Some incidents were easily handled, such as when Major Horsborough personally apologised to the Committee for his unseemly conduct and blamed his meeting 'an old friend from the East', when Captain Thompson was limited to one whisky and soda per day for the next three months, and when Major Kiellner-Davis had not even broken Club rules while engaging a room after licensing hours in order to obtain a drink. The misuse of the Bar at the Park Lane entrance by members arriving after closing hours was another matter and it had to be closed. The American Bar also caused problems, being blamed for three serious cases of drunkenness in April 1928, and it was decided to shut it at 8.30 p.m. Only one further significant comment appears in the Minutes, when the Committee discussed whether action should be taken over the conduct of a Club member and MP, Mr Garro Jones, who had spoken in the House of Commons on 21 March 1938 about 'the consumption of alcohol by officers of the RAF'. Jones's criticisms, however, had related only to conduct in officers' messes and not in the Club, and the Committee concluded that his statements were privileged and nothing useful would be served by making any representations.

Occasionally, too, there were incidents involving the staff. In April 1936 the Housekeeper complained that a member, recently returned from New Zealand, had invited three lady guests to his bedroom 'to see his trophies'. The member told the Committee that in his opinion the Housekeeper was drunk and had her facts wrong; there were only two ladies and they had spent only five minutes in his room. His explanation was accepted. A more serious and complicated issue in March 1937 occasioned a special Committee meeting to sort out a member's quarrel over an unpaid bill which had led to an allegation that the Secretary had struck one of the members. The Chairman, satisfied by the evidence of the Steward and other witnesses, concluded that the Secretary, Group Captain Burdett, had not been at fault.

At that time, day-to-day administration of the Club was the duty of the Steward, not always an easy post to fill. In 1929, however, an efficient Steward having recently been acquired, the Committee decided that the new Secretary now needed should be engaged primarily 'from a social point of view'; it was not essential for his qualities to embrace all aspects of Club management. The Committee, having decided too against appointing another ex-Army officer, also stated that the Secretary should ideally be ex-RAF, and with one exception this practice was followed until 1966.

Some of the early staffing problems that had to be addressed at less senior levels have already been touched on (pp. 31–2), but relatively low wages and poor living and working conditions made the Committee's task no easier in such matters. In 1929, a loss on the Provisions Account was partly attributed to the Chef not giving his best 'because he felt he was underpaid'; his salary thereafter was raised and he was promised a further rise if things improved. At about the same time the Head Valet's wage was raised by 5 shillings to £2. 7s. 8d. per week 'in view of ten years' service without any increase'. Some increases were across the board, partly in an attempt to compete with hotels whose employees were offered tips. Hours of work, too, were long – in 1924, for example, Still Room maids worked a 69-hour-week – and most staff were entitled only to 14 days' paid leave per year. Accommodation for some was available in the nether regions of the Club but was generally basic; indeed when in 1929 the boys' staff quarters were inspected by three Committee members they were 'horrified at the appalling conditions' and the Secretary was instructed to house them elsewhere.

Moreover, there was no staff pension scheme. When the desirability of one was recognised in 1930, it was clear that the Club's finances could not possibly support it. So the only way in which the staff's earnings could be supplemented was through the Christmas Fund. Relying on Club members' voluntary contributions, this provided for an annual payment graduated according to years of service and position, and ostensibly intended to compensate for the absence of tips. In 1936, the Committee agreed in principle to start a Staff Benevolent Fund to relieve cases of hardship among former staff or dependants. Being non-contributory, this would depend on voluntary donations from members, grants by the Club, and 10 per cent of all Club sweepstakes. With the worsening pressures of the international situation, however, the scheme went into abeyance. In 1939 it was restarted, and by December 1944, only one small claim having been made upon it, its assets stood at £2,000.

The approach of war had other implications. In January 1936 the Club sent two members of staff to a course of lectures run by the City of Westminster on anti-gas precautions and first aid for air raid casualties, several other members joined the Territorial Army and heard in May 1939 that they were liable for call-up, and in September 1939 the Committee was informed that the Secretary, Wing Commander Ogden, and eight other staff had been called up for service duties and three members of staff had qualified as Air Raid Wardens. At the same time six page boys and three kitchen boys had been evacuated on a Ministry of Labour Warrant. Certain protective measures were also taken: the Staff Recreation Room in the basement was sandbagged, the safest refuge in the building was identified as the basement between the staff lift and the wine cellars, and it was decreed that all baths were to be half-filled each night. The Club stood ready!

CHAPTER 4

THE WAR YEARS

Throughout the war the Club had the great good fortune to escape almost entirely the direct attentions of the German Air Force. Just conceivably it might not have done so had the Germans known what lay virtually beneath it. As today's members using the lower rooms may be aware from the rumble of underground trains, the Piccadilly Line runs directly below, and the former Down Street Station, whose entrance is still visible just round the corner and which had been closed in May 1932, was converted early in the war to provide secure emergency accommodation for the Prime Minister and his top-level colleagues. Churchill used 'the Burrow', as it was known by his inner circle, occasionally in the autumn of 1940, but it is most unlikely that its true purpose was known to anyone in the Club.

As for the Luftwaffe, its bombing in 1940 and 1941 was very largely concentrated in central and eastern London and little serious damage was caused towards the western end of Piccadilly. The worst incident was on 7/8 October 1940, when high-explosive and incendiary bombs were dropped near Hyde Park Corner extensively damaging the former residence of the King and Queen (when Duke and Duchess of York) at 145 Piccadilly, and blocking Hamilton Place and East Carriage Road. The Club itself suffered no more than occasional window breakages attributable to bomb blasts and anti-aircraft splinters; after four such nights between 16/17 September and 8/9 December 1940, the total repair costs were estimated at a mere £230. A further £14 sufficed to cover breakages on 16/17 April 1941, and the worst blow thus far came on 1 May when the War Damage Act compelled the Club to fork out £1,000 per annum for compulsory insurance. At the same time it was decided to appoint a member of the Committee to act as Air Raid Precautions (ARP) duty officer each night, and twelve valuable pictures were removed to Bentley Priory for safe storage. The insurance premium presumably paid its way in 1944 when on the night of 20/21 June a flying-bomb landed on St George's Hospital and knocked down a section of wall on nearby Constitution Hill. The front of the Club suffered minor blast damage and cost £1,500–2,000 to repair. The Committee formally thanked staff who had helped remove debris the following morning.

The Club's friendly relationship with its next-door neighbour, the Cavalry Club, was – not surprisingly – reinforced during the war. On 3 June 1940 Field Marshal Sir Philip Chetwode, its Chairman, wrote to the RAF Club on behalf of all its members expressing their profound admiration for the RAF's brilliant part in the recent fighting in Norway, Belgium and France; Colonel Bersey's cordial reply stressed that recent achievements were a magnificent exhibition of teamwork reflecting equally on all three Services. Soon afterwards, in September, the two Clubs agreed to help each other as far as possible in the event of air raid damage, but discussions with more distant clubs, including the Royal Aero and the United Services, concluded that mutual assistance would probably be impracticable. Nevertheless the RAF Club did lend a hand to some others on occasion, including the Public Schools Club in November 1940, the Royal Aero Club in January 1941, and the Naval and Military Club (the 'In and Out') in October 1941 after its members had lost the use of their billiard room.

So essentially it was 'business as usual' for the Club, but subject to a whole variety of practical constraints imposed by the pressures of war. One of the overriding factors was the substantial increase in the number of members – and others – wanting to use its facilities. Statistics contained in the Annual Accounts for 1943 give the measure of this, comparing the average number of meals served per year in 1938/9 with those served in 1942. Breakfasts rose from 7,250 to 11,999; full lunches from 25,851 to 29,808; quick lunches from 11,834 to 18,907; and dinners from 13,186 to 20,075. Overall these increases represented an almost 40 per cent growth in trade and for the rest of the war the Club operated at virtually full capacity. In so doing it had to cope with growing difficulties both in obtaining the necessary provisions and in retaining and recruiting sufficient staff of acceptable quality.

For the first few years the Committee Minutes contained little reference to food shortages other than to record the government's introduction of rationing on 8 January 1940. Since bacon and ham would be limited to four ounces per head per week, and butter to a sixth of an ounce per person per meal, it was decided to acquire a bacon slicer and a butterpat machine to enable accurate amounts to be served. Sugar was among many other rationed commodities, and in November 1940 the Committee went so far as to record its thanks to a recent visitor, a RAAF wing commander, for his gift of a 28lb case. Not until 1942, however, did the situation really start to tighten, with the Meals in Establishments Order limiting the courses that could be served and laying down maximum prices. The first major issue in the Club arose late in 1943, when the Secretary reported that the Food Office – part of the inevitable wartime bureaucracy – had drawn attention to a shortfall of 930 'points' coupons and 160 tea coupons and requested the names of the delinquents. Since the members concerned had broken the law the Committee decided to ban them from residence until their arrears were cleared. The worsening effects of food rationing were illustrated at the 1944 AGM. The meat ration, valued at threepence per head in 1940, was now less than a penny; the Club's allowances of cheese and fish, both unlimited in 1940, were now 13lb for cheese and 73lb per day for fish.

It is quite remarkable that the Club managed to cope with the rationing system as well as it seems to have done, though the 1943 AGM did witness a substantial debate about the reasons why an egg brought in by a member and having been bought for tuppence, the Food Minister's controlled price, should cost him threepence to have cooked. Only in 1944 did specific suggestions and complaints begin to appear. The Chef, asked to serve boiled suet pudding, was told by the Club's butcher that extra suet was very difficult to obtain. Then the Steward reported that smaller portions of meat would have to be served in the Dining Room if every member was to receive a portion. In January 1945 the meat allocation was slightly increased, but the meagre supply of poultry was still inadequate, and in February so serious were the food supply problems that the Steward explained them to the Executive Committee at great length, stressing the shortages of meat and poultry and the poor quality of the bread. Moreover, unrationed items were not available in sufficient quantities to supply lunch as well as dinner. On 24 May, shortly after VE Day, the situation was even worse; rationed foodstuffs were being further cut, as were various non-rationed items such as pork pies, down by 60 per cent, and smoked salmon, which had virtually disappeared from the market. Lobsters and oysters, however, were still available, though they had to be sold at a loss!

Dwindling supplies of liquid refreshment also caused concern in the later war years. A two-man sub-committee, formed in February 1942, reported that since stocks of all kinds of liquor were declining it had authorised price increases, imposed limits on daily issues, and shortened bar hours. In October 1943 port rationing had to be introduced; it would be available after lunch and dinner only on alternate days and never on Sundays. At the same time Colonel Bersey did a deal with the Club's wine merchants to exchange a small surplus stock of hock and burgundy for gin, and in March 1944 whisky supplies were in serious decline: against monthly consumption of 344 bottles, only 240 were being received and the monthly issue had to be cut to 204. Thereafter, thanks to the negotiating skills of the Secretary and other Committee members, stocks were kept more or less steady, and members were enabled to celebrate the events of 1945 without significant restriction.

How best to keep the Club properly staffed was another major preoccupation for the Committee. In 1938 there had been 120 employees but by March 1940, due very largely to the call-up of some and the evacuation of others, the strength was down to 92. By March 1942 it was a mere 77. Recruitment of replacements inevitably proved very difficult and in 1941, in an attempt to remedy this 'acute shortage', the Committee agreed to raise rates of pay, especially for waitresses and housemaids. Soon afterwards the Chairman suggested that valets – who had little to do after 11a.m. – should help out under-staffed departments whereupon one with 22 years' service refused: 'he would rather resign'. A year later Bersey summarised the situation, reporting that 'changes of staff and difficulties of replacement had increased substantially, the actual turnover during that time being no less than 160'. The higher wages demanded, and readily obtainable, were creating many anomalies, with some new staff being paid more than many of comparatively long service. In 1943 the continuing problems led to the introduction of a Wartime Staff Gratuities Scheme, under which sixpence was added to overnight charges and meal bills (threepence for quick lunches). The total was then pooled among all staff except the Secretary and Accountant, and eventually, by the end of the war, each employee was receiving some 10 shillings per week.

The replacement of staff livery, particularly waitresses' clothing, also became increasingly urgent. In 1943 the Association of London Clubs raised the subject with the Government, but to no avail, and in May 1944 the Committee enthusiastically followed up Staff Chaplain McHardy's suggestion to purchase black-out material (which was coupon-free) so that the Club Tailor could make overalls for the waitresses. The idea had to be smartly dropped when the Committee heard that such use was illegal, and the waitresses were left to make do for another year.

Committee discussions in 1944 illustrated some of the other practical issues. In one particular month, for example, ten basement porters were engaged and all left after a few days, not because of pay and conditions but because they were 'the tramp type'; no others were available. For waitresses the problem here was wage rates and tips: the Club paid £2. 13s. per week, including bonus, whereas local restaurants offered half as much again. Such costs were prohibitive – and would compel the Club to concede equivalent rises to other staff. To make matters worse, young recruits all too often left for more profitable employment once they were trained. The Club premises as a whole were suffering too. As the Steward told the Committee, the building was very dirty and untidy because of staff shortages, and while he had a very high opinion of the Chef and his assistant, the kitchens too were seriously undermanned. Sadly one of the assistants discredited himself, after nineteen days at work, by breaking into the Staff Canteen, stealing the Cellarman's £4 wages, and turning on the taps of two full firkins of beer; he was later arrested in Shrewsbury on another charge.

There was, of course, another side to the picture, for the Club would never have coped without the loyal, dedicated work of many of its staff, some of whom had served it well from its very earliest days. On 26 April 1945 the Committee paid special tribute to one of them, agreeing to grant £50 ex gratia to the Chef, who because the kitchen had been understaffed for many months 'had worked far beyond the scope of his normal duties'. The Committee went on to describe the Dining Room as saturated, not simply because waitresses were unobtainable but because, even if they were found, the kitchen was so under-staffed that it could not increase the number of meals served. And all this at the moment when the European war was virtually won!

The steadily increasing wartime pressure on the Club's facilities had not surprisingly caused serious congestion and the imposition of restrictions. In April 1942, for example, so great was the number of meals being required in the Ladies' Dining Room that the staff could not keep tables reserved for the frequent late arrivals and it was therefore decreed that no dinner bookings would henceforth be accepted; it would be 'first come first served'. From October 1943 onwards no member would be able to invite more than one lady to lunch or dinner. Then in April 1945 the Committee took the extreme measure of withdrawing members' privilege of introducing lunch guests other than in the Ladies' Dining Room. Soon after this staff shortages and supply problems forced the Committee to go even further in proposing that for the time being the Club should elect no new members at all; henceforth the number elected would be determined by the number of meals the kitchen could provide. In fact no further members were elected between 12 April and 26 July 1945, by which time the waiting-list stood at 107.

Two other measures deserve recording. In 1942 bedroom charges were substantially raised and the number of rooms available for permanent (i.e., three-months) and semi-permanent (i.e., one month) hire was reduced; in 1943, thanks to heavy demand augmented by overseas visitors, eight weeks' notice of termination was given to all existing tenants and strict rules on 'period renting' were introduced. Then in 1944 restrictions were imposed on wedding receptions. In future they would require Committee approval: the Club would not provide food, liquor or flowers, or 'incur any expense', and 'a fair proportion' of the guests must be members.

While regulations such as these were easily enforceable, one wonders how far it was practicable to apply the various dining and drinking rules fairly and to ensure that the entry of non-members, including ladies, was kept under control. Inevitably there were limits to what could be done by the hard-pressed staff, particularly at busy times, and in 1942 the Committee expressed concern about the unauthorised use of the Club by non-members. Some non-members who remember those days certainly used it on occasion for a drink or a spot of lunch. It was a most important informal meeting place for many of the senior officers serving in the Air Ministry or visiting London, and as such was certainly providing a worth-while return to the Royal Air Force for the support it provided.

Notwithstanding all the practical difficulties, the Club's massive expansion of trading came to be reflected in its overall financial position, though during the first couple of years the outlook had been far from promising. Indeed, the trading accounts ran in deficit up to the end of 1940, but the situation was in part retrieved by the reduced staff costs, the landlords' agreement to halve the ground rent, a 10 per cent fall in the rateable value, and an increase in the bank overdraft. As Bersey told the AGM in March 1940, 'so far we have held our own ... it will need the efforts of the Committee and everyone else to weather the storm'. The turn-around began in 1941 when the trading profit was called 'exceptionally good', and in 1942 the revenue account went into credit at £1,769, reflecting the 80,000 meals served that year as compared to 50,000 in 1940. In 1943 and 1944 the annual credit balances came out at £7,427 and £6,410 respectively, while the annual demand remained steady at around 85,000 meals.

The winter of 1942/3 was also marked by an event of historic significance. As Bersey reminded the Committee on 29 October, a Deed dated 8 October 1928 had embodied Lord Cowdray's original intention (see p. 14) to allow the Club the option to buy all the shares of the RAF Club Company at par; since this option would expire on 24 February 1943, he suggested that the Committee should take it up. There was unanimous agreement to go ahead and to appoint the Club Chairman, Deputy Chairman and Vice-Chairman as Directors. Then, Bersey having left the room, Air Vice-Marshal J. J. Breen, Vice-Chairman since April 1942 (and serving in the Air Ministry as Director General of Personnel), paid him the highest possible tribute for his work throughout the entire life of the Club and proposed commissioning an oil painting for presentation to him. So 1 January 1943 witnessed a packed Extraordinary General Meeting, described as 'A coming of Age Celebration', which reported the acquisition of the shares and heard the Colonel's account of the Club's origins and history. After paying tribute to the previous Chairman and the Committee, he concluded:

> Remembering all these, and particularly the 453 original members who are still with us today, I am very proud and happy to say to you; 'the Club is now yours. Uphold it, be jealous of its reputation, and guard it well'.

Bersey then made presentations to 19 members of staff each of whom had been in the Club's service for between 18 and 25 years. Now it was his own turn, as Breen paid him fulsome tribute, calling him the Club's 'mainspring and driving force', and presented him with his own portrait, painted by Cuthbert Orde. This now hangs to the left of the front entrance, flanked by the certificate that many Club members signed at the time.

This occasion turned out to be the high-point in Bersey's years as Chairman. He had in effect exercised direct personal control of the Club's major affairs ever since Wing Commander Ogden's departure as Secretary in August 1939, when he had turned down two volunteers as replacements and asserted that the Club's administration was being carried out quite satisfactorily. Ogden, on retiring from the RAF, was welcomed back in April 1940, but died in January 1941, whereupon the Committee accepted Bersey's offer to double as Secretary for the time being; four months later Major C. P. Radclyffe-Dugmore was appointed.

Nor for several years was there an Executive Committee; despite a weekly pattern of meetings having been arranged by its Chairman in September 1939, it never met and not until September 1943 was it re-established. Meanwhile authority to deal with the many day-to-day issues hitherto its responsibility was vested in Bersey as Chairman of the Main Committee. This Committee itself was not easy to run. Serving officers in particular, for obvious wartime reasons, were hard to recruit and then to retain, and since many seemed unable to get to meetings sufficiently regularly, attempts were made to insist on minimum rates of attendance. The procedure for filling the frequent vacancies, too, was a cause of dissension between the Committee and Club members who objected to co-option.

So for much of the war the Club was for most practical purposes run by Bersey, and one of the most important issues that engaged his attention was membership. Surprising as it may seem to later generations but understandable under the conditions of the time was the restrictive approach to the size of membership. On 1 January 1940 this stood at 2,222 (it had been 2,141 in 1939). It was down to 1,980 a year later, up to 2,324 in October 1943, and peaked at 2,347 in January 1945. Anxieties about the initial decline – caused partly by war casualties – may have influenced a suggestion at the 1940 AGM that officers joining the Club for the duration of the war might be offered a reduced subscription. Bersey scathingly demolished this, saying that such men had long been eligible and there was no reason for them now to come in at lower rates than the 2,000 who had supported the Club over the peacetime years. A more far-reaching proposal arrived in November 1941 in a letter from Air Vice-Marshal H. V. Champion de Crespigny, who wanted pilot and flying officers of all branches of the RAF to be admitted as Temporary War Members. His idea was accepted in January 1942 insofar as commissioned aircrew (flight lieutenants and below) were concerned, but the Committee declined to open the doors to officers of other RAF branches. Membership of the Club was to remain, as it had always been, the preserve of the practising airmen. At the same time a Life Membership scheme was ill-advisedly introduced, with subscriptions determined by applicants' year of election, and by 1945 some 188 such elections had been made.

Other major steps forward were taken in 1943. In April Bersey delivered some trenchant observations on the motives of members who had joined since the outbreak of war. The memorandum he wrote reminded its readers of the purposes of Lord Cowdray's original gift, stated that the Club was not a 'philanthropic institution' or a 'hostel' for the RAF, and insisted that it was for use 'only by its elected and contributing members'. Too many of the new members, most of whom were wing commanders and above, could and should have joined long before, and too few young members – essential to the future life of the Club – were applying. Accordingly, Bersey went on, they were now to be offered new inducements, including reduced subscriptions and bedroom charges, and the absence of the entrance fee which was being reimposed for officers older than 23 and above flight lieutenant rank. The sequel to this came in October, when the Committee decided that the election of serving RAF officers should be free of any limits for the time being, irrespective of age or Service duties; there would be a waiting-list for non-serving officers. So it was that the aviators' monopoly of membership was removed, though what would eventually prove a momentous decision seems to have passed almost unnoticed if the virtually static membership figures are anything to go by.

The war had also brought with it various new categories of members. On 11 January 1940 it was agreed to offer 'Dominion Status' to officers of the Royal Canadian Air Force, the Royal Australian Air Force, the Royal New Zealand Air Force and the South African Air Force. They would have no voting rights and be members for the duration only, but to signify how welcome they were would pay only half subscriptions. In November the Under-Secretary of State for Air, concerned at the plight of many of these young officers, asked the Club to give them an initial free period, followed by only a nominal subscription. Although the Committee did not accept the free period, it did offer a further reduced rate for the first year. At about the same time similar privileges were granted to officers of all Allied Air Forces on nomination by a senior Air Ministry officer, and in January 1942 this privilege was extended to officers of the United States Army Air Force. By the end of the war 211 Dominion and 37 Allied officers had been elected. Occasionally too, special membership was accorded to distinguished 'air personalities', as for example in September 1943 when Sir Robert Watson-Watt, 'the father of radio-location' (or radar), was invited to become a subscribing member.

As the war neared its end the Committee turned their minds back to the classes of membership that would afterwards be appropriate, and a Sub-Committee led by Air Marshal Breen, still Vice-Chairman, reported in April 1945. Their task, as they saw it, was to assess the significance of the major changes in the RAF officer corps brought about during the war and try to reconcile these with the importance of preserving the aims and traditions of the Club. It was not an easy task for a group of senior officers who had been brought up in 'the old school'. As they stated in their preamble:

> It has been necessary in recent years to commission for non-flying duties many individuals who by normal standards would not have been considered suitable for officer rank. If the Club is to maintain its appropriate social status it may well be that some of these ... may not be altogether suitable for membership of the Club. It is therefore desirable to define more precisely what our aims are now to be as regards membership.

The primary aim which then emerged was based on the assumption that large numbers of officers receiving permanent commissions in the post-war RAF would wish to be members. Steps must therefore be taken to ensure that the membership ceiling – whatever this might be, for it would depend on changing conditions but must be above 2,600 – was not reached. It followed that the Committee must not elect 'large numbers of non-flying types whose connection with the RAF had been extremely short, and whose experience of flying or anything directly connected with flying had been negligible'. The primary aim must be to acquire young General Duties officers.

To this end the Sub-Committee devised a complicated formula designed to ensure that applications for membership could be allotted priorities according to Branch, seniority, type of commission, practical flying connections, and so on. An application form was drafted with a long series of questions, including 'Are you of British nationality?' and 'Are you of pure European descent?' Within three months the Election Sub-Committee reported that the scheme was not working as intended –

hardly surprising! Clearly there was more thought to be given, and it next recommended the adoption of an age criterion, namely that two-thirds of the candidates elected at any one time were to be aged below 35, irrespective of rank.

The same Sub-Committee, oblivious of any inconsistency, was also far from sure whether all officers commissioned for flying duties were necessarily suitable; these doubts were brought out when it was required to rule on a suggestion that RAF officers holding the Victoria Cross be given Honorary Life Membership. It came down firmly against. While the main Committee certainly had the power to elect in this way persons who had rendered signal service to the RAF, it did not follow that all holders of the VC would be acceptable as members, or for that matter be of pure European descent. In any case, it concluded, such officers were eligible for ordinary membership if suitable.

In other ways too the Club was trying to look ahead. When on 9 March 1944 the Committee received the audited accounts for the previous year, it agreed to follow up Bersey's recommendations for post-war repairs and renewals, thus taking advantage of £11,000 which had accumulated for such purposes in the Club's reserves. Bersey's report pointed out that eight years had passed since the last four-yearly overhaul and redecoration, and it would be another two or three years before the material, plant, labour and so on became available. In addition some of the Club equipment (e.g., heating, refrigeration, cooking) was decrepit, and the total outlay he estimated at some £21,000, which revised arrangements with the Prudential should help to meet. The Committee unanimously agreed to commission the detailed planning and costings.

A year later, by which time the Repairs and Renewal Reserve stood at £13,500, Bersey submitted what he called his Ten Year Budget, in which he forecast the number of members needed to support the Club's finances. He thought the present membership of 2,460 would rise to 2,600 in 1952 and remain steady thereafter, and that the current annual per capita income of £16 per head, yielding roughly £35,000 per year, would continue. This would cover the present rate of expenditure, to which must be added annual 'Beveridge' payments of £450 to provide staff pensions, and £600 to build up a Lease Redemption Fund in readiness for the eventual expiry of the Club Lease in 2019. On this basis, after a few 'lean years', the Club's finances would, Bersey predicted, be healthy.

It would be wrong to conclude at this point that all was sweetness and light. Indeed, according to the detailed minutes of the 1944 and 1945 AGMs, there were many dissentient voices. In March 1944 a former RNAS airman, Wing Commander V. R. Gibbs, speaking as a previous Committee member (he had been responsible for the Club's badge collection), sharply criticised the Committee's management of its financial surpluses and its excessive profit-taking on meals. 'Either we are being overcharged or are not getting value for money ... the catering, which is the personal respon-sibility of the Secretary, is not in the hands of a competent person ... the menus are appalling'. Strong views were now expressed on both sides. For example, a self-proclaimed 'plain-spoken Yorkshireman who liked good grub' asserted that he got 'damned-sight better food in the Club than anywhere else' and wondered if the critics were used to feeding at the Savoy. In contrast trenchant criticisms were directed at the Club staff, including the Head Waiter in the Members' Dining Room, who was accused of extreme rudeness.

This led Air Commodore J. L. Vachell (a respected figure who had been Air Attaché in Berlin before the war) to a direct attack on some of the Club officials. The Secretary, Major Radclyffe-Dugmore, was far from suitable and it should be possible to find a retired RAF officer who would be popular with members and could first be given some training in another Club; the other Service Clubs were far superior to ours, which was just about the dirtiest place he had ever been in. As for the Chef, he could neither cook nor carve, and he wrote menus in bastard French. Vachell's closing words were reserved for the Chairman himself:

Colonel Bersey has rendered most valuable service to the Club ... but he has one drawback as Chairman ... he is too strong a character. The impression conveyed by the staff is that nobody else counts in this Club. I go into the Dining Room ... it is full ... but there is one vacant table with the chair turned up ... I am told it is reserved for the Chairman. We are in this war to get rid of dictators, but I suggest we get rid of our own dictator first. Colonel Bersey has done a great deal of work for us ... but I think he should be replaced before we get tired of him.

There were elements of truth in these strong words, but not surprisingly the Committee rallied round and at their next meeting on 13 April unanimously expressed their appreciation of all Bersey had done over the years and asked him to continue his duties. They also firmly dissented from Vachell's remarks and disapproved of the circumstances in which they had been delivered. Bersey nevertheless heeded the warning, stating that as soon as there was a suitable replacement who could devote the necessary time to the affairs of the Club he would wish to resign.

The tensions between the Committee and a section of the membership remained apparent at the 1945 AGM, which Bersey chaired for the last time. He was able to deal with some of the criticisms when explaining his Ten Year Budget (see p. 50) and most of the other protests related to less major matters. It was disgraceful, for example, that the entrance door to the Club could not be closed and partly as a result the building was full of draughts. On one significant issue, however, Gibbs returned to the attack. Co-option of Committee members was, he thought, occurring increasingly often and he proposed that the procedure should take account of members who had stood unsuccessfully for election at previous AGMs. The Vice-Chairman objected to this: it was necessary to be able to invite individuals to serve for their particular skills and the members who had elected them should show confidence in the Committee's judgement. Gibbs retorted that the Club was not part of the Air Ministry and it did not follow that because one held high office there one would automatically be a good member of the Club Committee. Gibbs' proposal received 24 votes to 19 but not quite the necessary two-thirds majority. It had been an acrimonious debate, showing that the depth of feeling on this and other matters was still there.

Shortly afterwards, Bersey wrote to the Secretary tendering his resignation, saying that he knew many wanted a serving officer as Chairman, and the Committee discussed this on 12 April. While they would have liked him to continue they felt it advisable to change 'owing to the feeling in the Club amongst certain members'. Air Marshal Breen (now Head of the Post-War Planning Executive in the Air Ministry) was therefore elected to succeed him and Bersey replaced him as Vice-Chairman. So for another year Bersey continued to fulfil a major role overseeing the Club's financial management. On 28 February 1946 he produced his final financial report, stressing that while the Club remained in net surplus the catering and bedroom departments were showing substantial losses; they ought to be self-supporting and not depend on the Bar and subscription incomes. He concluded:

This is my last report, and my many years of experience of Club finance impel me to say: 'Elect members while they are keen to join, make all the profit and build up reserves as much as possible while the opportunity remains. I am no pessimist but I know that the most difficult period and problems in the history of the Club are in the future and perhaps not too far distant'.

How right he was. For almost the first 30 years Colonel Bersey had dominated the Club. His knowledge and experience of it were unrivalled, and he had done his utmost to ensure that the first Lord Cowdray's vision for it should be fulfilled. Eventually – and probably inevitably – his strong personality and self-assurance had made him difficult for others to work with and now it was certainly time to go. With equal certainty the Club will always remain deeply indebted to one of its greatest figures.

CHAPTER 5

THE POST-WAR SCENE

At the end of 1945 a host of questions faced the Royal Air Force, not least of them the future shape and size of its officer corps. Contraction was inevitable, and the extent of the Service's post-war commitments meant that, once again, a great many officers would be spending much of their time overseas. Moreover the General Duties Branch would now concentrate largely on flying duties, with substantial numbers of officers undertaking the essential support tasks as members of specialised ground branches. At the same time, with many of the wartime officers departing, the recruitment of junior officers as both aviation and other specialists was going to be difficult and much reliance would have to be placed on the soon to be introduced National Service scheme. Such an uncertain environment was far from conducive to careful, thorough thinking about the future, and the RAF Club was just one of many Service-connected organisations which had to run their affairs and make their plans in greatly changed circumstances. So it is hardly surprising that an institution still largely patronised and administered by its 'old guard' should have concentrated initially on trying to keep it running along traditional lines and on preserving its own special ethos.

At its head the Club had a new President, Marshal of the Royal Air Force Sir John Salmond, a former Chief of Air Staff and always a wholehearted supporter. He held the post for the next 23 years until his death in 1968. In the chair, having taken over from Bersey, was Air Marshal Breen, and ever since then the Chairman has been a serving Air Officer, holding the post usually for one, two or three years. Some of the elected Committee members, including the Vice-Chairman, have stayed on the Committee much longer, and the full-time post of Secretary, usually filled for several years at least, has been central to the efficient running of the Club. The Committee system as it has developed in more recent years is discussed in Chapter 8.

The last Army officer who served as Secretary, Major Radclyffe-Dugmore, seems to have attracted considerable misgivings which gave rise to calls for his replacement, preferably by a retired RAF officer. So in 1946 the Committee listed the qualities required – for example good appearance and manner, good education, tact and good mixer, unmarried or widower, under 55, business acumen – and soon afterwards Radclyffe-Dugmore handed in his notice. Then on 16 January 1947 'Londoner's Diary' in the *Evening Standard* reported that several hundred Club members were petitioning the Committee to appoint a professional Secretary, 'who would know all about the ins-and-outs of catering'. The first RAF officer to hold the post, Squadron Leader E. E. Hardie, who had recently returned home after four years as a prisoner of war in the Far East, was duly selected on 1 May.

The challenges facing the Committee at this time were not just those posed by the changing RAF; they related too to the straitened circumstances of the nation as a whole. Indeed, life in the later 1940s was harder in many ways than it had been during the war, with the rationing of food and other essential commodities such as clothing becoming more stringent, and severe shortages occurring in other areas including fuel, building materials and skilled labour. The Chairman summarised the situation to the 1947 AGM. The past year had been a struggle against every sort of shortage: staff, consumer goods, food and drink, labour and building materials, linen and crockery. To these he added the refusal of the Board of Trade to issue clothing coupons for the purchase of staff livery, the inability of the GPO to renew worn-out telephone equipment, and much more. As for repairs, priorities had to be assessed in terms of what could be done without closing the Club and things which did entail this; and in any event no contractor could give firm start and finish dates or avoid interminable delays.

The supply of food was inevitably one of the Club's greatest problems, with even potatoes and bread on the list of rationed items at times, and many other 'essential' as well as luxury items hard to come by. In February 1946, for example, the Committee was told that no rice had been received since March 1945, only 30 ounces of bacon and ham were available per person per week, there were no prunes or Spam, bad weather had stopped supplies of shrimps and lobsters for a month, and bread – cut thinly – would be served only on demand. In July 1947 the stock of tinned foods was fast running down. During 1947 and 1948 meat, poultry and fish shortages were reported, and the overall effects by now were to reduce the number of meals being served. Exacerbating the catering problems were fuel restrictions: in February 1947, for example, the Ministry of Fuel and Power prohibited the use of electricity at certain times, thus preventing members having their own bacon and eggs cooked after 9 a.m. or being served afternoon tea before 4.30. At the same time the Club heard it would receive no coal for some weeks, whereupon 20 tons of logs were purchased.

To make matters worse, the Club was still having to comply with the Meals in Establishments Order, originally introduced by the Ministry of Food in 1942 to limit the prices chargeable for meals in restaurants, clubs and similar establishments. With commodity prices rising this caused serious problems, as for example in 1945, when lobsters, which could be readily purchased so as to help out with the meat ration, had to be sold at a loss. In 1947, however, the Club managed in part to circumvent the restriction by creating a Private Dining Room for members who reserved tables at least a day in advance. The Order was abolished in 1950 and the last forms of rationing ceased in 1954 with the freeing of butter, cheese, margarine and cooking fats.

Nor were liquor supplies sufficient during these years, and when in June 1946 the Committee discussed the impact of measures to ration its consumption they decided to discontinue 'doubles'. Then in 1947, when the government decided to increase the export of the country's available whisky supplies from 50 to 75 per cent, the Committee realised that the Club's reserve would be exhausted in six months, and immediately cut the cellar issues. Gin supplies, however, remained adequate and from 1950 onwards the Committee seems not to have needed to concern itself with the practicalities of slaking members' thirsts.

Another major problem in this post-war period was recruitment and retention of staff. Not only did the Committee wish to bring the total numbers back to pre-war levels, but they were particularly keen to raise the proportion of men to women. These were not easy tasks. Requests to Labour Exchanges and private employment bureaux achieved very little; advertisements in newspapers as far afield as Scotland yielded hardly any suitable applicants; considerable efforts through the RAF Association and other old comrades' organisations were largely fruitless, not least since the kind of people wanted had to receive considerable training to bring them up to Club standard; displaced persons, though enthusiastic, proved quite unsuitable; and there were now – partly thanks to the raising of the school leaving age – few young boys coming forward for training. Insular attitudes towards foreigners also played their part: in July 1947 the Manager stated that staff reluctance to employing displaced persons would be eased if the Club were allowed to take on half-a-dozen for domestic work, in which case they could be segregated for accommodation and messing purposes. There were, too, growing problems of staff retention, thanks to the higher wages on offer in central London hotels and the appeals of better paid seasonal employment – exacerbated by the Club's policy of no tipping. The Club's servants depended on the Christmas Fund to compensate, which of course it did not. All in all, staffing was a constant anxiety, not made easier to bear by members' complaints about standards of service. Nor did the Catering Wages Act (which came fully into force on 1 January 1948) help with its rules about the length of the working day, minimum rates of pay and overtime rates. Such difficulties were of course shared by other Clubs, with three of whom the RAF Club introduced in 1949 a rota for closure on public holidays when triple rates had to be paid.

Under all these circumstances it is hardly surprising that the Club's membership remained almost static. Indeed, as the AGM was informed in 1946, congestion in the Club, staff shortages and limited supplies were forcing the Club to restrict elections of new members and continue to operate a waiting-list, with two-thirds of the available places going to officers under 35. However, in November 1947, given the prospect of declining usage of the Club, the waiting-list was eliminated by the election of 72 new members, bringing the total membership to a record figure of 2,615. This, wrote the Chairman, was a healthy situation but he went on to emphasise that the Club's reputation depended almost entirely on the type of candidates admitted to membership: indications were not lacking that some members had little idea of how to behave, and he proposed that all future candidates should be formally proposed and seconded, with supporting personal information, by members of at least two years' standing.

The Chairman's optimism about membership numbers was hardly justified when, a mere two months later, the Committee decided to recommend an increase in subscription, i.e., the entrance fee up from 10 to 15 guineas, town members' rates 10 to 12 guineas, and country rates 7 to 8 (see p. 23); bedroom charges too would rise. The reasons were understandable given the Club's operating position, its growing wage bill and the need of a substantial programme of repairs and development which had been under discussion for some time. In fact the only profitable source of revenue was the Bar, and an overall deficit of £1,040 was now forecast for 1948.

Five years later the Club Auditor, Squadron Leader H. V. Barham (a former accountant officer), summarised the Club's overall financial situation at this time. 1942–7 had been prosperous, leading to reserves of £15,000 plus £25,000 set aside for deferred repairs, and with current assets exceeding liabilities by £29,000. The next five years in sharp contrast had seen the £15,000 reserve becoming a debit balance of £4,000, and the £29,000 becoming a deficiency of £13,000 (see p. 59). So it was in the winter of 1947/8 that the Club's finances started their long decline towards the red, and the decision to raise subscriptions – seemingly taken without much thought for its likely adverse consequences – provided the defining moment. On 29 July 1948 the increase was notified to members; by the end of that year resignations totalled 138, compared with 60 for 1947, and from then until 1953 total membership averaged only just over 2,500 per annum, with recruitment merely balancing wastage. The subscription rise had achieved virtually nothing.

The lesson was not lost, and when a further 3-guineas increase for town members was suggested in January 1950 it was firmly rejected in Committee and the AGM duly informed. From now on the membership sub-committee concentrated its activities on ways of attracting specific categories of new members, particularly Cranwell cadets, and other young officers at concessionary rates. Officers of the United States Air Force (USAF) serving in the UK, together with officers of Dominion, Colonial and other Allied Air Forces, including students studying on RAF training courses, were also offered some form of membership, usually temporary or honorary.

There were too some special cases. In September 1949 Lord Trenchard, who had recently resigned his ordinary membership on financial grounds, was elected an Honorary Life Member. A month later Sir Archibald McIndoe, of 'Guinea Pig' fame, became a paying member in recognition of his distinguished service to the RAF. Then in April 1950 many Committee members, somewhat concerned that two members of the Air Council who were not Club members were about to be offered Honorary Membership, failed to persuade the Chairman to invite them to apply for membership in the normal way and thus give their own Club tangible support.

A particularly significant long-running question also surfaced at this time. The status of ladies in the Club had throughout its history been a matter for debate, but it was in 1947 that it was first formally raised with the Committee by Commander Lord Gifford, who suggested that a new category of Associate Member be introduced which would accord them use of the Drawing Room and 'the privilege of ordering tea'. Nothing specific seems to have happened as a result, but in 1949 the Secretary showed his awareness of the need for better ladies' amenities when he suggested that an American-style cocktail bar be installed in the Ladies' Lounge. Younger members, he said, complained about aged and unattractive waitresses who were entirely unskilled at mixing drinks, and also the need 'to walk the plank under the often critical and inquisitive eyes of the older members and guests'.

That was the year when on 1 February the creation of the Women's Royal Air Force, replacing the WAAF, gave its officers full commissioned status and in September 1951 the Chairman, Air Marshal Sir Alan Lees, raised in Committee the possibility of granting them Associate Membership: 'it would be very contentious' he said, 'but should not be dismissed out of hand'. In November the Committee backed him. While there might be objections from members on grounds of female 'infiltration', they believed sufficient safeguards could be put in place. In February 1952, however, the Vice Chairman (Air Vice-Marshal A. C. Sanderson) opposed putting the proposal to the AGM, on the grounds that the only reason for having ladies in was financial and the AGM would probably reject it. The Chairman stuck to his guns: eligibility should be extended to any commissioned officer connected with the Air Force. So on 31 March 1952 the question was put to the membership at the AGM. The Chairman declared that other Clubs, including the 'In and Out', had taken the plunge without harm, and went on to assert that strict conditions would be in place to keep the WRAF to the ladies' side of the Club. The old guard would have none of it, a paltry six members voting in favour.

While on the one hand a significant move to extend the Club's membership and thus its business was being firmly rejected, on the other its overall financial situation was already causing much concern. In August 1951 the Secretary had set out the position as he saw it. Whereas the Club needed an annual trading profit of £3,500 to be on a sound footing, at present the trading balance was barely in credit and the bank overdraft was approaching £12,000. Action was urgently needed, he said, but since cutting overheads was virtually impossible and efforts to increase membership were proving impracticable, he returned to increased subscriptions and other charges as the only answer – and at the same time inviting the 187 Life Members, who had enjoyed several free years, to subscribe again. Over the next nine months the Committee devoted much time to considering such measures as raising bedroom charges, admitting Army and Navy aviators (as well as the WRAF), instituting with other Clubs a further rota of weekend closures, and altering the layout and use of some of the Club's facilities in order to economise. Much attention was also given to the reasons for the continuing decline in catering profits, variously attributed to high staff costs, high prices, poor organisation and inadequate control.

Very little had been achieved by June 1952 when Wing Commander B. T. Aikman – a qualified accountant newly appointed to oversee the Club's Finance Sub-Committee – reported that the total deficit was now £16,000 and went on to describe the Club's overall position. Apart from its furnishings and fittings, the Club's fixed assets were the leasehold premises which under the Town and Country Planning Act could be sold only as a Club and were worth £87,000.* By 2019 when the lease would expire, that sum would have gone and in the absence of a sinking fund the Club's Profit and Loss Account was misleading. Moreover, since the overdraft was secured by the lease, the time was not very far away when the Bank would ask for it to be paid off. 'If we consider the Club as a private venture company, the Directors would say it was going bankrupt and not so slowly either.' Since the Club could neither sell out nor drastically cut expenses, Aikman concluded, it must undertake an energetic sales promotion drive, since it was 'in no way near capacity for sleeping, feeding and administering drink to its members', and also improve its facilities and services so as to induce members to spend in the Club rather than elsewhere. The Committee endorsed this, and among other measures the Chairman, Air Chief Marshal Sir James Robb,† wrote personally about the Club to all station commanders. Such measures had little effect and in October Aikman produced a further memorandum underlining his frustration at the failure to proceed with the agreed capital improvements without which operating losses would continue.

---

* Had the building been sold for other purposes before the Country Planning Act was passed it would have been worth £245,000 and the Committee lodged a claim for £158,000 as recompense for this loss. Eventually, and not surprisingly, this got nowhere, but for some while the Committee naively hoped it might solve their problems.

† Robb had just retired after serving as Chief of Staff to General Eisenhower during the war, then Vice-Chief of Air Staff and finally CinC Air Forces Central Europe.

By January 1953, doubtless tired of recommending action to remedy the Club's finances, to improve its catering facilities and RAF image, and to increase its membership (a target of 3,500 new members was being mooted), he withdrew from the Committee 'for reasons that need not be gone into' but which almost certainly reflected disagreement with the member who now replaced him.

This was a 47-year-old qualified lawyer, Wing Commander Peter Reynolds, ably assisted among others by Squadron Leader Barham. On 8 January the Sub-Committee (soon to become the Permanent Finance Advisory Committee) recommended increasing the subscription and 'a virile policy of increasing membership and utilisation of the Club'; alternatively other premises should be acquired in keeping with the Club's present income (a course of action which would be legal, said Barham) or the Club should affiliate with another one. Were the present rate of losses to continue, added Barham, the Club would not survive in its present form and in its present buildings for more than three years. Once the Club's finances were balanced, however, an insurance policy should be taken out to provide for redemption of the Lease. The Chairman stressed that the Club had the capacity for 5,000 members, almost twice the present 2,587, and the idea of closing it one day a week in association with other Clubs would be considered. Significantly this idea had been mooted in The Times on 18 December 1952 in an article about the financial problems of Clubs in general; the RAF Club was not alone in its difficulties.

In February 1953 Air Marshal Sir Hugh Walmsley, who had recently retired after serving as CinC Flying Training Command, entered the fray, expressing confidence that much could be done within the Service, especially among junior officers, to raise the membership. He was willing to write to Commanders-in-Chief and had already spoken to the Air Member for Personnel, Air Chief Marshal Sir Francis Fogarty, who would assist where possible. Reynolds, too, was busy, reporting first that the Royal Aero Club would not be averse to discussing affiliation, since their premises were too small. He then suggested amendment of the membership rules so that serving officers would only require their CO's recommendation, a simplification that would greatly facilitate the recruiting drive. At an Extraordinary General Meeting called for this purpose on 30 April, this proposal was carried unanimously. Meanwhile, on 15 April, Reynolds, accompanying the Vice-Chairman,

Air Commodore W. G. P. Pretty*, and others, had discussed the membership drive personally with AMP, who agreed to write to all Commanders-in-Chief himself and to endorse letters from the Club Chairman to all unit commanders. This was the first time since November 1918 that the Club received official backing from the Air Council.

The scene was now set for Reynolds to fire his bombshell and try to persuade the Committee to reverse all that had been said in the past about subscriptions and reduce those payable by the 984 serving members. The rates for the 1,600 retired officers would remain unchanged. Some 500 new members would be needed to balance the loss, so if altogether 2,000 came in the Club's finances could be well on the way to solution. After lengthy discussion on the principle and detail, the lower rates were agreed and publicised, with a new brochure being circulated in September, and by November 1,300 new applications had been received. At the same time there had been strong protests from the retired members and at an EGM on 3 December the reasons for the decision were explained and the members irresponsibly told that the hoped-for substantial increase in membership would eventually allow all subscriptions to be lowered.

The Finance Committee had already been considering how to use the extra subscription income to help rescue the finances, and since Reynolds recognised that his ideal targets of 3,000 new members and a 10 per cent increase in Club usage were unlikely to be achieved, he felt it essential to make substantial savings on the one area of expenditure where economies were possible, i.e., catering wages. To this end major structural alterations to the kitchens and dining rooms were essential. Consideration of the necessary plans in early 1954 – including the possibility of placing the Club catering out to private contract – soon led to a growing rift between the cautious and the bold. The former, following Barham's lead, pointed to the continuing losses, the still rising overdraft, and the annual £1,718 cost of the Lease Redemption Policy that had rightly just been taken out with Guardian Assurance. This was not the moment, they argued, to spend some £15,000 on alterations to the building. The latter, inspired by Reynolds, who stated that the kitchen needed to be modernised anyway, urged that the Club should take 'a

---

* Pretty, at that time Director of Electronics Research and Development, subsequently served as Director General of Organisation, CinC Signals Command (1961–4) and Deputy Chief of Defence Staff, Personnel and Logistics (1964–6).

business risk' and build on the growing success of the bold membership policy already adopted.

One significant alteration did take place however. Following a recommendation by Painter Bros (kitchen equipment experts) that all cooking and serving of food should be concentrated on the Ground Floor, it was decided to relocate the Dining Room to the Smoking Room on the Ground Floor, and to switch the Smoking Room to the First Floor in its place. These changes were implemented in 1955, and the Duke of Edinburgh attended a Cocktail Party to mark the opening of the new Dining Room on 9 December.

Meanwhile by April 1954 the Committee discussions were indicating a guarded optimism. New membership applications were approaching 2,000, the trading loss had fallen to almost nil, and the Chairman, now Air Commodore Pretty, wrote to AMP outlining the financial situation and raising questions of an Air Ministry loan or grant to pay for the alterations. Replying in June, AMP could offer no help but remained very interested in the Club's welfare and would look into the matter again towards the end of the year. Meanwhile with the trading account showing continued improvement – and favourable comments appearing in the national press about the Club's recovery – Barham was predicting that it would soon be all square. Nevertheless, in early 1955 the counsels of caution were again being heard and in April Reynolds felt it necessary to summarise the achievements of the Finance Committee over the past two and a half years. The Club's annual losses had fallen to about £5,000; membership had more than doubled; the Club usage had risen by some 10 per cent; and proposals to reduce the £5,000 deficit by £4,000 had just been put to the AGM. Yet shortly afterwards, on 1 June, Reynolds resigned from the Committee. As the Chairman, Air Vice-Marshal S. R. Ubee, then recorded, he had been 'a very active, forceful and constructive member during difficult times', and he presumably went because he was unable to persuade his colleagues to push ahead with further measures which he deemed essential. Reynolds' contribution to the Club was, however, far from over, for he then became its legal adviser.

Surprisingly, despite the all-out campaign to increase the membership, the opportunity to reinforce its success by admitting ladies had not been seized. Indeed, AMP himself had reopened the debate in February 1954, telling the new Secretary, Wing Commander S. P. A. Bousfield, that the issue must be faced if the Club was to move with the times. The

Committee had mixed views. Some observed that the Naval and Military, Royal Thames Yacht and Royal Aero Clubs had already successfully introduced Associate Membership for ladies; others feared increased congestion of the existing ladies' facilities. Despite a 7/4 informal vote in favour, the Committee pusillanimously took no action on the grounds that such a proposal should emanate from individual members, not the Committee. Clearly the Secretary, now Group Captain V. G. A. Bennett, felt strongly about this for in the autumn of 1955 he urged the Committee to admit WRAF officers and members' wives as Associates, and added the Guards to the list of other Clubs which were already increasing their business through operating such schemes. The Committee, following the lead of yet another new Chairman, Air Marshal the Earl of Bandon,* would have none of it and again the issue was shelved.

How, one wonders, was the Club viewed by the large numbers of younger officers who were now being persuaded to join? One who came in was Tom Moulson, a pilot in 601 (Auxiliary) Squadron who later emigrated and eventually rejoined the Club in 2002. He clearly recalls the Main Bar with its pewter tankards and its aero-masculinity, the squash courts, the hall area with its dignified desks and wonderful RAF Club notepaper, the lavatories below, the entrance by the side porter's door, the stuffy silence of the large front Reading Room where he read the papers. The atmosphere was certainly heavily traditional; by no stretch of imagination was it a young man's club. Yet this did not seem to matter much; in those days one respected Air Force seniority because it was associated with the pioneers of flight and the heroes of war. For him there were three appeals: the obvious practical advantages, an affinity with the RAF, and the mystique of leather-armchair gentlemen's clubs that gave one a sense of having moved up. The idea that the Royal Air Force Club would have him was probably a source of snobbish pride. Others were less impressed. A former Cranwell cadet recalls, on being shown into the Smoking Room, seeing a portrait of a senior officer on the wall, with the officer himself sound asleep beneath it. Then, on entering the Bar he was immediately accosted by a member anxious to sell him insurance!

The squash courts, as Moulson remembers, were among the Club's more significant amenities. With the upper court in need of repair after

---

* An Irishman widely known throughout the RAF for his unconventional behaviour, Paddy Bandon always rejoiced in his nickname 'The Abandoned Earl'. He ended up as an Air Chief Marshal.

Her Majesty the Queen, by Denis Fildes

Visit of King George V
and Queen Mary to the
Club, 14 March 1922

HM Queen Elizabeth The
Queen Mother signing the
Visitors' Book, 3 June 1997

Viscount Cowdray,
by William Orpen

Below: Lieutenant
Colonel W. C. Bersey,
by Cuthbert J. Orde

Below right: Air
Vice-Marshal Sir
Sefton Brancker, by
John Lavery

The Triptych, by Frank Wootton

Wellingtons in Action,
by Mark Bromley

Halifax B111 limping
home on three, by
Frank Wootton

Setting Course,
Outward Bound, by
Alan Fearnley

Above: Peenemünde, by Frank Wootton. Below: Operation Manna, by Alan Fearnley

the war, they had at first been little used and takings were far from meeting costs, but with growing activity the Club team was good enough by 1956 to head the Third Division of the Bath Cup Competition. Billiards and snooker competitions too resumed in 1946, but ten years later the room was no longer in demand and was converted to a Snack Bar – soon to become the Gentlemen's Bar – as part of the reorganisation then being undertaken. Maybe significantly, the Club had acquired its first television set in 1951 and installed it in today's Drawing Room. As for golf, also a significant pre-war activity, nothing at all happened until 1957 when the Chairman started discussions with the Moor Park Club. Nor did outside events attract much support. In 1950 the Club's request to be allowed to erect a marquee for its members at the Farnborough Display was rejected by the Society of British Aircraft Constructors (SBAC) on the grounds that every visitor was its guest, and in 1953 the Committee dropped the idea of a Club enclosure at the Queen's Coronation Review at Odiham on the grounds that the space allocated was too far away. The celebration of the Coronation itself was a different story. Planning for a viewing stand taking 452 people had started in September 1952, and by December 309 members had applied for 1,183 seats at 12 guineas each, including bed, breakfast and lunch; 105 applications had also been received for four large bedrooms which would be set up as viewing rooms at 100 guineas each. The Club's exploitation of its wonderful position on the processional route finally brought it a profit of £2,700.

The one major annual event which the Club did try to establish was a New Year's Eve Dinner and Dance. Although the idea was first mooted in 1946 it was not until 1950 that the first one took place. In 1948 the Club's closure for renewal of the boilers had caused cancellation, and in 1949 – after the Committee realised there would be no liquor licence after midnight thanks to New Year's Eve falling on a Saturday – the Ball was switched to Twelfth Night and then cancelled when only 78 tickets had been sold. The success of a General Election Dance on 13 March gave more encouragement, and the first New Year's Dance took place on 28 December 1950, making a profit of £41 – hardly a success story. Three years later, hoping to cash in on the influx of younger members, the Committee tried again but failed to recognise that most young officers possessed neither dinner jackets nor tails, that wearing Mess Kit in the Club was contrary to Queen's Regulations, and that most of them would not be in London anyway on New Year's Eve. Further provisional plans fared no better, encountering staff problems and the unavailability of the Central Band, but in December 1955 the plans were more successful and from then until 1960 the function filled an important position in the Club calendar.

The Committee also devoted some attention to the ambiance of the Club, and particularly its trophies and paintings. The last of the pre-war game trophies which had adorned the Club in such numbers were removed from the Billiard Room in 1947 and further offers refused, but several aerial artefacts were accepted. Then came the portrait of Winston Churchill, painted by Cuthbert Orde from sketches he had made some time previously. It was unveiled in 1950, Churchill having declined the invitation to do this himself. Soon afterwards the Committee turned down a proposal from members to erect a Battle of Britain Memorial, judging that the most appropriate 'memorial' would be paintings of aircraft flown by all Commands during the war, financed by members' contributions – a policy which the Club has tried to follow ever since (see Chap 11). Subsequently, in 1953 the increasingly important badge collection was re-arranged; the first 150 squadron badges to have been received were displayed along the first-floor corridor and the rest in the American Bar and Oyster Bar.

So by the mid-1950s the doubling of the Club's membership and the widely perceived improvement in its finances seemed to be bringing hope for the future, but, as understood by those who were in the know, they marked merely a lull in the storm. Much worse was to come.

CHAPTER 6

INTO THE ABYSS

It was in January 1956 that one of the RAF's most charismatic Chiefs of Air Staff, Sir Dermot Boyle, arrived on the scene. None of his predecessors, apart from Trenchard and Salmond, had ever shown much interest in the Club, but Boyle, the first Cranwellian to hold the office, had always been a keen supporter and for the rest of his life would exercise his considerable influence on its behalf. As CAS, among the biggest problems he had to face were the consequences of the prediction of the Defence Secretary, Duncan Sandys, in the 1957 Defence White Paper that the advent of the missile would mean the end of the manned fighter aircraft. Boyle saw this as a challenge to the very existence of the RAF, and his inspired handling of the subsequent crisis in RAF morale was one of his greatest achievements. Not surprisingly, he appreciated the value of the Club in this context and encouraged the Air Council to take a more active interest in it than hitherto, but the overall 'Sandys climate' was certainly not conducive to improving the Club's position relative to serving officers as a whole in the later 1950s. Indeed, in 1962 Boyle's successor as CAS, Sir Tom Pike, actually resigned his own Club membership – hardly leaving him in a position to encourage his subordinates to give it their backing, or indeed to persuade some of his Commanders-in-Chief even to join.

By this time the Club was in a truly parlous state, as implied in a critical article that appeared in the William Hickey column of the *Daily Express* in January 1956, saying that it was poorly organised and losing money. The optimism of 1955 was quickly evaporating, as the record membership figure of 5,120 in January 1956 slipped to 4,974 in 1957 and continued to decline. As might have been expected, the considerable number of younger officers who had joined were not bringing proportionately increased business and such was the fall in weekend trade that it was decided to close the main Dining Room at weekends – a move which saved staff but was hardly calculated to improve the Club image. Yet a year later this measure was reversed so as not to inconvenience young members who could visit only at weekends. At the same time, the Secretary was reporting that 90 per cent of the staff were constantly changing, which underlined the problems of running the

Club and maintaining a good standard of service, and he was authorised to raise wages by 10 per cent in order to reduce the differential with other Clubs. This cut little ice when £7.10s. per week was on offer elsewhere compared with the £5.10s. which was all the RAF Club could afford. The vital area of Club catering suffered particularly; in September, for example, the Committee learnt that three catering managers had been employed in 18 months, and now the Chef had left for a higher-paid post.

Against this depressing background, it was decided in March 1956 to return the subscription rates to their former levels at the end of the year, it being assumed that the resultant additional income would more than offset the likely resignations. So from January 1957 non-serving members would pay the full Town or Country rates of 15 and 10 guineas respectively (the latter applying outside a 20-mile radius of Central London), while serving officers' subscriptions would be graded according to rank, ranging from 15 guineas for group captains to 3 guineas for flying officers and pilot officers. Unsurprisingly, the Committee's optimism proved unjustified, not least since some members simply continued to pay the reduced rates and eventually had to be faced with expulsion. A flight lieutenant who did resign stated that he considered the new rate of 6 guineas an uneconomic proposition and went on: 'raising the subscription after the Club had increased its membership on the strength of the 1953 Brochure seems tantamount to using a decoy to attract fresh game into the range of one's guns'.

The blinkered approach of the Committee at this time is illustrated by some of its membership decisions. In February 1956, for example, an application form from a non-serving officer elicited the opinion that it was not sufficient for him to have held the King's Commission and been duly sponsored; his social and business standing should also have a bearing on his suitability. A subsequent application from a squadron leader who worked as a master tailor was only accepted after some debate and the Chairman lamely decreed that each case must be determined on it merits. Age was another issue. In 1958 the Secretary expressed reservations over the election of a 64-year-old officer, believing it not in the Club's best interest to accept new candidates 'at this very mature age'; on the Chairman's casting vote his application was rejected. Soon afterwards a 67-year-old wing commander resident in New Zealand was turned down for full membership despite being very active in aviation matters and always helpful to RAF visitors. Two more followed: a group captain aged 63, and an air commodore of 54 who had applied for membership only after retirement. In 1959, a 64-year-old's application led the Chairman to observe that some members in their advancing years had become a little embarrassing, and a senior Committee member to add that a person who had waited 40 years before seeking membership should not be accepted. The Committee thereupon ruled that sponsors of candidates aged over 60 would be required to provide additional information and that age would in future be a factor in dealing with applications. Such ageist attitudes persisted into the early 1960s – and all this despite the 1954 Committee having done its utmost to appeal to officers from as far back as the RFC.

The blinkers were also on elsewhere, for example in relation to officers of the United States Air Force, substantial numbers of whom were now based alongside the RAF in the United Kingdom. In 1958 the RAF commander at Greenham Common, who asked if they could become eligible for membership, received a dusty answer. The rules did not permit it, the USAF had its own very good club in Bayswater, and the younger members whom the RAF Club was keen to attract were 'already a little sensitive of the higher spending power of some of the older and more senior members'.

The most serious membership question, however, remained the status of ladies in the Club. The regular trickle of members' complaints about the misuse of certain facilities illustrated the difficulties. In 1956, as a case in point, a lady had been seen using the telephone box in the Members' Cloakroom, whereupon a notice was displayed in the Ladies' Cloakroom stating that they MUST use the first-floor and not the ground-floor corridor. Their use of the squash courts was also queried, and while the Committee accepted that ladies could use them in the mornings, they decided against posting notices to this effect 'because players objected to them'. The appearance of young ladies in the Ladies' Bar and Lounge wearing 'skin pants' also aroused comment, prompting the Committee to deprecate this tendency in a West End Club and ask the Secretary to write a personal letter to the host member – if he could be identified. In 1957 a more significant issue arose when some members asked for ladies to be allowed to use the Piccadilly Entrance rather than Park Lane, thus avoiding the long trek upstairs and then back downstairs to the Dining Room. The Committee opposed this because 'it would alter the whole character of the Club', and it took the nearby disruption occasioned by the construction of the Piccadilly Underpass a few years later to resolve the issue. Ladies having then been permitted as a concession to use the main entrance, in 1962 the Committee rejected a member's subsequent proposal to return to the status quo ante, though the ladies would still be asked to avoid using the ground-floor corridor. Another divisive issue surrounded the provision of double rooms for married members, a proposal favoured by the Chairman, Air Vice-Marshal Maurice Heath, and approved at the 1957 AGM. It was then opposed by the Executive Committee on the dubious grounds that members would object to wives breakfasting in the Dining Room, that they might remain in the Club while their husbands were out at meetings, and that the Ladies' Lounge would have to be open throughout the morning. The General Committee, accepting its commitment at the AGM, compromised by stipulating that the ladies must breakfast in the Oyster Bar. It would be some time before the necessary double rooms could be provided.

Other facilities, too, caused problems. In 1958, following adverse comments on the presence of ladies in the TV Room, a second set was installed in the Ladies' Lounge, leaving the TV Room for men only. In 1959 the Committee rejected several suggestions from Air Vice-Marshal Sir Gilbert Nicholetts (one of the RAF's better-known pioneer aviators) for additional lunching and dining facilities for unaccompanied ladies. Next year they turned down a request from Lady Hudleston (the wife of VCAS) for the 'Wives of Allied Air Forces in London' to hold their monthly get-together in the Club; the Rules, they replied speciously, required all guests to be accompanied by the host member, only a member could pay for drinks, and such a function would be very unpopular with most members. In March 1961 it was a different story when Sir Dermot Boyle met the Secretary to convey a request from his wife, Chairman of the RAF Officers' Wives' Association, to hold their Annual Tea in the Club. He explained that all the ladies were wives of RAF officers, many of whom would come along afterwards 'and it would become a very good jolly'. Despite expressing a ritual caution about the restricted facilities available, the Committee could hardly refuse!

The Club was still, however, making no attempt to tackle the fundamental question about the presence of ladies. Successive Chairmen seem to have recognised that a ladies' membership scheme was bound to come sooner or later, but believed that it would be so controversial in the face of much entrenched opinion that it could not be rushed. So when Associate Membership for ladies was sympathetically discussed in December 1956, the Committee agreed that the 1957 AGM, as in the past, would overwhelmingly reject it. At the AGM itself there was considerable discussion, at times acrimonious and even puerile, and the Chairman, Air Vice-Marshal J. G. W. Weston, concluded the sense of the meeting to be 'definitely against'. Moreover, some of the Committee felt, such a scheme could well lead eventually to full membership for WRAF officers, described as 'a regrettable development'. In 1958 a new dimension was added when Flying Officer M. E. Darling, a serving woman medical officer and thus commissioned in the RAF, not the WRAF, applied for membership. The Committee evaded the issue thus posed and in turning her down simply stated that the Club was unable to accept ladies as members.

During the next few years the pressure eased, but in 1962, with the Club's financial situation very much worse, Air Commodore W. I. C. Innes (then AOA Coastal Command) launched a proposal to admit WRAF officers as members and wives of members as Honorary Members. He argued that since most officers were now married they usually came to London with their wives, and the wives came more frequently than their husbands; there would therefore be considerable increase in the use of the Club. The Committee, chaired by Air Commodore A. V. R. Johnstone, decided to support admission of the WRAF but not the wives, on the grounds that the Club lacked the necessary facilities. At the AGM on 22 March 1963, Innes and his seconder, Air Commodore R. H. C. Burwell, stated their case more strongly than it had ever been argued before, but to the expressed horror of many members at the prospect of a 'gaggle' of females in the Club, and the proposals were soundly defeated. The old-style Committee returned to the subject for the last time in January 1964, when Johnstone told them that he thought the Club would soon be asked by the Air Council to admit the WRAF as members and wives as Associates. While still opposed to having the wives, the Committee agreed by a large majority to accept the WRAF officers and also the officers of the Princess Mary's RAF Nursing Service. At last, apart from Wing Commander Reynolds, the Committee now seemed determined to grasp this particular nettle, albeit under pressure from outside.

The Air Council had been showing interest in the Club in several other ways. In May 1956, under Boyle's leadership, it announced its willingness to help and requested details about what the Club itself was doing to solve its problems. Based on the answers provided, AMP wrote to all Commanders-in-Chief stressing the urgency of increasing the membership and seeking further ideas; in consequence of this letter, and a parallel letter from the Chairman to Station Commanders, the Committee was told in February 1957 that more interest was now being shown in the Club than at any other time, with Service receptions of various kinds particularly prominent. Among the suggestions that had been received one was for a Junior Officers' Bar, which the Chairman said the Club could not afford not to implement – provided it was not 'mixed'. Another proposal was for 'block mess subscriptions' which would enable up to ten officers from a particular station to use the Club at any one time – an idea firmly rejected since it would risk a substantial falling-off in the number of individuals paying full subscriptions. At the same time the Air Ministry responded to the Committee's request for a £28–30,000 grant to help pay for much-needed improvements, but only came up with a 'once and for all' gift of £7,500 (drawn from the Prize Fund), which did no more than reduce the overdraft from £31,000, as recorded in the 1958 accounts. Concerns about the growing overdraft were also reflected when the Committee discussed in 1957 whether to continue paying for the Lease Redemption Policy and agreed to do so at least until 1960, when the surrender value would equal the total premium then paid.

So towards the end of the 1950s, while the Club's overall financial situation was becoming ever more desperate, the Committee went on clutching at straws and consoling themselves with thoughts that other Clubs – including the Cavalry – were also facing problems. Moreover there were many external pressures over which they had no control: dock and bus strikes, car parking restrictions, increasing coal and electricity prices, higher wages and pension contributions, and many more. The way in which the Committee itself operated did not help. In 1957 it had been unable to identify an acceptable full-time Secretary, whereupon one of its own members, Group Captain J. H. S. Richards – a former accountant officer – had agreed to serve in an honorary capacity on receipt of an annual honorarium. Hardly a satisfactory arrangement, this gave rise to various disputes, and one particularly long-serving Committee member, Mr Walter Noble, was an outspoken critic to the extent of opposing the election of Air Marshals as Chairmen, since they knew nothing about the Club – though he would be prepared to accept

Air Commodore John Searby since he actually lived in the Club. Soon afterwards Noble questioned the need for a Club Manager, whereupon the Secretary came to the Manager's defence and stated that 'this continued subversive hostility to the management, from a small section of the membership, was contrary to the best interests of the Club'. The Chairman subsequently felt it necessary to stress the importance of unity in dealing with uninformed critics and of giving the Secretary the Committee's full support. While Mr Noble afterwards resigned, clearly the Committee was not working together as it should.

The most fundamental weakness, however, was identified in March 1961 after it had been decided to appoint a full-time Secretary. A former RFC airman, Sir John Austin, then suggested that the Club should look for a businessman, only to be told that the Committee had already agreed to employ a retired RAF officer. While he might not be a specialist in catering and so on, his task would be 'to coordinate all functions under the direction of the Committee'. Just conceivably, had Austin's ideas been pursued at that point, the disaster facing the Club might have been averted. As it was the newly appointed Secretary, Group Captain A. V. Rogers, took over in May 1961 and did his very best, but the task was to prove beyond him.

Already, in June 1960, the bedroom charges – well below hotel rates – had been raised, but in January 1961 proposals to increase catering prices and subscriptions were deferred. Then in March, having agreed to spend £3,500 in painting the outside of the Club, the Committee turned to the renovation programme which had for so long been on ice and included such essentials as re-wiring and plumbing as well as internal redecoration and refurnishing of the main rooms. In June, after these measures had been costed at £8–10,000, they again had to be deferred in favour of an 'immediate face-lift' of the Club entrances, the Ladies' Lounge and the Cocktail Bar, for which estimates were to be obtained. Meanwhile the Committee had been embarrassed when a Club member, Wing Commander Ramsay, personally approached the retiring Chairman of the RAF Central Fund* asking about a grant to help the Club. The Committee's unanimous reaction was that the Club should stand on its own feet; if it

---

* The Central Fund, which is administered by AMP on behalf of the Air Force Board (formerly the Air Council), takes charge of all non-public funds that are surplus to the immediate needs of the RAF, including those from units which have closed. It can make grants and loans, inter alia, to charitable, philanthropic and benevolent organisations in accordance with Charity Commission regulations.

could not do so, said Air Commodore D. M. Strong, it would be better to fold up. However, although the Committee considered a grant would be unbecoming, they started to think that a Central Fund loan might be another matter. Meanwhile in July – in an attempt to prime the pump – Sir John Austin offered to donate £100 to the Club provided 99 other members did likewise.

Austin's well-intentioned offer had little chance of taking off in the atmosphere of those days when too many members were unenthusiastic about the way the Club was being run. After 1960, for example, the New Year's Eve Dances were either cancelled or not even planned because of lack of support; attempts in the late 1950s to organise lectures by well-known personalities came to nothing, and in the sporting domain the golfing society virtually died and only squash kept going, albeit with only slight support. Just two social functions are recorded: a cocktail party to welcome the Duke of Edinburgh on 9 December 1955, and a luncheon in July 1960 at which the Club entertained members of the RAF Escaping Society and their Resistance guests, 110 in all. The Committee, in generous mood despite the parlous finances, provided a full lunch, including wine, free of charge. A much less arguable item of expenditure at this time was a portrait of the Queen. Unsuccessful attempts having been made in 1956 to obtain Her Majesty's agreement to sit for this – understandably since she was being inundated with similar requests – the Club decided to pay 200 guineas for a copy of Commander Fildes' portrait on display at the Imperial Defence College, and this was hung in the Club during the autumn of 1961. Several paintings were donated at about the same time, including a second portrait of Sir Sefton Brancker and one of Sir Frederick Bowhill. Other ways of encouraging pride in the Club were, however, rejected. Back in 1950 the idea of designing a Club Flag had been dropped, and in 1956 the Committee unanimously decided against introducing a Club Tie: it would be of no financial benefit, it was unnecessary to advertise the Club in this way, and such a tie 'could be worn by any Tom, Dick or Harry'.

Not surprisingly the Club continued to attract its share of incidents, usually involving bouncing cheques and unseemly behaviour, and not all these were attributable to members. In 1956, for example, a non-member used a member's name to cash several stolen cheques, so the Secretary and House Manager devised a scheme to detain him should he reappear. He did and was detained, whereupon the police found that he had defrauded 23 other London Clubs and Rugby Clubs of £1,260, for which he spent three years in prison. In 1958 another fraudster was intercepted; known as 'the Commander' and a regular gatecrasher, he had been caught cashing a small cheque and was then found to have conned several other Clubs. Together with regular losses of members' property, such incidents demonstrated that security was inadequate; as the Secretary commented, 'anyone could walk into the Club and take a lift' and 'staff knew only a fraction of the current 4,700 members'. The Committee, however, though told that other Clubs now had membership cards, was disinclined to issue them at this juncture.

Nor did staff dishonesty help. In 1954 a hall porter, acting as a bank messenger, absconded after collecting £98 from the Bank, and in 1959 a night porter, assisted by a stoker, also made off taking with him cash and night drinks. This and similar occurrences led the Committee to employ only members of the Corps of Commissionaires for such duties. Most staff, however, conducted themselves loyally, even though there was no proper pension scheme. There was not even provision for gratuities for those with long service; in 1959, for example, the Secretary asked for recognition of three bar staff who were about to complete a hundred years' joint service, only to be reminded that this would set a dangerous precedent and be unfair to other personnel who were less in the public eye. Private subscription raised £85 for them. Then in 1964 the retirement of Jim Griffin, the particularly long-serving senior barman, was marked by Sir Dermot Boyle presenting him with a barometer, accompanied by an honorarium and a small pension, all paid for by members' donations. This seems to have been an exceptional event. More generally, relatively few members were prepared to contribute to the Christmas Fund, the scheme whereby the Club tried to compensate staff for the prohibition of tipping, and the Club simply could not compete in the local labour market where most hotels and restaurant workers were better paid and receiving substantial gratuities.

The early 1960s were indeed depressing and worrying years. The Committee had in reality done little more than tinker with the fundamental issues facing the Club, and in October 1961 came the final body blow. Squadron Leader V. O. McQuillan, chairman of the Finance Sub-Committee, had been to discuss the Club's redecoration and repair programme with the bank manager, only to be informed that as a consequence of the Chancellor of the Exchequer's credit squeeze, Head Office wanted to halve the Club's overdraft limit to £15,000. When McQuillan said that the programme would probably need a £25,000 limit the manager asked for full details of the Club's requirements and its proposals for increasing its annual revenue. Reporting this grim situation to the Committee on the 11th, he persuaded them to accept a very limited redecoration and repair programme (which at least included the rewiring), and to generate extra funds by raising subscriptions, increasing all bedroom and house charges, instituting a membership drive, and applying for a grant from the Central Fund.

Coupled with these potentially disastrous measures, McQuillan suggested that the Club follow the lead recently given by the Royal Aero Club, which had sold its Lease with only ten years to run. Pointing out that the Lease on 128 Piccadilly still had 60 years to go, he went on to present an enticing prospect, namely that a developer would pay the Club £300,000 or more for the Lease and accommodate the Club within the new building for a peppercorn rent. Notwithstanding that the Club would thus be selling its birthright, the Committee authorised him to pursue the matter. Almost immediately the Cavalry Club began to consider joining the discussions, since simultaneous redevelopment of the two sites could enhance the value of both leases. At the same time, it was agreed to tell the present Lord Cowdray what was afoot but only as a matter of courtesy, since his forebear 'did not present this actual building'. The Club's original benefactor would have turned in his grave!

So in 1962 there followed discussions with the Club's Solicitors, Simmons and Simmons; the commissioning of Russell Diplock Associates to prepare a scheme for replanning the site; and its submission to the London County Council. The LCC, having initially wondered whether modernisation of the site would be preferable, accepted redevelopment. Then, in 1963, the Committee consulted Sutton Estates, the owners of the Freehold, who undertook to give sympathetic consideration to the redevelopment – though they would not extend the existing lease. Coutts Bank, the Club's neighbours, were next on the scene with an offer to lease part of the existing building for £4,000 a year, whereupon Watney Mann entered the fray by suggesting that they and Coutts should jointly redevelop the site. There followed a series of meetings between the Club, Diplock, Coutts, Watney Mann and the LCC, culminating in February 1964 when the LCC accepted the comprehensive redevelopment that was being proposed, stipulating that the elevations must be of the highest quality and would need the blessing of the Fine Arts Commission.

It had taken more than two years to bring the redevelopment proposals thus far, and with the Committee unbelievably hoping that the scheme would provide the answers to the Club's problems, they had failed to take account of the rapidly increasing pace of its decline. At the end of 1961 membership stood at 4,285; a year later it had fallen to 3,901. The overdraft, notwithstanding the bank manager's earlier strictures, had risen in 1962 from £15,642 to £24,592, and Club usage had markedly declined. By December 1963 further resignations had cut the member-ship to 3,808 and the overdraft had climbed to £37,097. By the end of 1964 membership had dropped to 3,372 and the overdraft stood at £47,118.

Now – at long last but far too late – the Committee began to face the true gravity of the situation. As Reynolds put it, 'the Club is completely insolvent, we are losing £5,000 a year (much more in fact!) and doing nothing about it'. Supported by Group Captain Richards, Reynolds then became chairman of a new Finance and Development Sub-Committee, which quickly concluded that the redevelopment scheme as envisaged would provide no real financial benefit. Only 50 years now remained on the Lease, the Club would be left with only 21 double and 21 single bedrooms, and no provision had been made for the economics of transition, including the cost of temporary accommodation during the redevelopment. That scheme was a dead duck. What the Club must now do, they went on, was first to increase the net revenue by £15,000 per annum – not by increasing membership or admitting WRAF officers, to which Reynolds remained adamantly opposed – but by substantially raising subscriptions and increasing food and bedroom charges by 20 per cent. The long-term aim, they proposed in July 1964, should be to replace the present building with a new six-storey block; the Club would occupy part of it, with facilities sufficient for 2,000 members, this being the maximum space a developer would be willing to allocate. All one can say about the new building plan is that it belonged in the world of fantasy and could not possibly have been endorsed by yet another new Chairman – of whom there had been far too many since the end of the war.

The decision to offer the post to Air Marshal Sir Walter Pretty, now back in the Air Ministry, had been made in April after contentious argument about the respective merits of serving and non-serving officers for that role. The Chairman ought to be drawn from the Committee, some said, but since Pretty was already experienced in the post others argued firmly for him. Eventually, with one strongly dissentient voice, the Committee agreed on 6 May to co-opt him and appoint him Chairman. In agreeing to take the job on Pretty can hardly have been unaware of the Club's desperate situation and the need to take a grip on it. Things had got no better, however, when he chaired the Committee on 22 October 1964 and had to endorse the subscription rises about to be announced in the Club Bulletin. At the same time he listened to a series of lame ideas from the Membership Committee about means of increasing the membership. One particular suggestion may, however, have made him sit up. It came in a letter from a member shortly due to return home from SHAPE, Group Captain Neil Cameron. Having served on the Committee for five months in 1963, he realised only too well that it lacked the ability and vision to deal effectively with the Club's appalling situation, and was now offering to form and lead a sub-committee of serving officers to consider ways of stimulating membership among their contemporaries. Group Captain Richards, quick to appreciate the possible significance of this, proposed Cameron's co-option to the Committee. Perhaps it was not yet too late to revitalise the leadership and set the Club to rights.

CHAPTER 7

THE COLONELS' REVOLT

One evening in October 1964, two of the RAF's most highly rated senior officers, both serving in Paris on the staff of the Supreme Allied Commander Europe, were returning home to Versailles after visiting the French military officers' club, the Cercle Militaire. Air Vice-Marshal Bob Hodges was Air Executive to the Nuclear Deputy; Group Captain Neil Cameron was Personal Staff Officer to MRAF Sir Thomas Pike, the Deputy Supreme Commander. In the taxi their conversation turned to the RAF Club, from which they had just received the bulletin announcing a major increase in subscriptions. While both were already aware of the Club's failing fortunes, the situation it revealed was clearly life-threatening. By contrast in the Cercle Militaire, a club to which every officer serving in the Paris region was required to belong, the atmosphere was so much more welcoming, and not just to officers but also to their families. Might it not be possible, they asked themselves, to change the Club image and require every RAF officer to join? If so, even with the most modest level of individual subscription, the Club's problems would be solved.*

If their ideas were to have any chance of success the two officers knew they must move quickly. Cameron, who had already heard that he was soon to return home, on promotion, to become Assistant Commandant at Cranwell, wrote to the Club offering to chair a new membership sub-committee and was duly co-opted (p. 78); the two of them then began 'networking' their many influential friends and building up support for a special Club meeting. One who immediately came aboard was Group Captain Freddie Sowrey, CO at Abingdon, who was first invited by Air Vice-Marshal Denis Smallwood to put his name down for a 'Colonels' revolt'.† Very soon Hodges had the 40 signatures he needed, and on 19 November he wrote to the Club Secretary protesting personally and on

* This episode is described on pages 137–9 of Lord Cameron's autobiography *In the Midst of Things*, (Hodder and Stoughton 1986). It was actually drafted after his death by Henry Probert in consultation with Sir Lewis Hodges.

† The title of this Chapter is derived from one of the phases in the political turmoil in Greece after the war. There was a military coup in 1967, followed by a right-wing dictatorship of the Greek Colonels until they in turn were overthrown in 1974. At the time, the Press was constantly referring to 'the Colonels' and the early stages of their dictatorship coincided with Hodges and Cameron's ideas for the salvation of the Club.

behalf of many other members against the subscription increases and requesting an extraordinary general meeting. The President (Sir John Salmond) and Vice-President (Sir Dermot Boyle) were sent copies. Sir Walter Pretty replied personally pointing out that under the Rules the only way to cancel the increase before it was due to come into force at the end of December was for the Committee itself to call such a meeting, and this was now being done. Pretty understood the urgency of the matter and was determined to waste no time.

So 14 December 1964 saw 147 members attending one of the most critical gatherings in the history of the Club. Called ostensibly to confirm the Committee decision to raise subscriptions, the meeting was opened by the Chairman, who explained in detail the financial situation and the inescapable need to increase revenue in 1965 by £15,000. The stage was thus set for Bob Hodges who, having disclaimed any intention to subvert the Committee's responsibilities, presented the case for deferring the increase until a thorough exploration of the alternatives had been achieved. The large number of resignations either actual or pending the outcome of this meeting, he said, was a measure of members' adverse reactions, and all too many were from the serving officers who represented the Club's future; how many of these would it take to nullify the benefit of the subscription increase? The Committee, he tellingly observed, had accepted the arguments against such a policy as recently as March, and it was hard to understand how circumstances could since have changed so radically. He therefore advocated suspension of the increases and the formation of a small working group of serving officers to investigate urgently means of attracting large numbers of serving officers into the Club. Of the 20,000 officers in the RAF a mere 1,700 (8.5 per cent) were at present members; if this percentage were doubled subscriptions could be held steady, if quadrupled they could be halved, and the wider implications were enticing. Having already written along these lines to Commanders-in-Chief and received most favourable responses, he stated himself willing to set up such a group.

Twenty-two members contributed to the ensuing lengthy and at times emotive and heated discussion. Most were strongly or cautiously supportive of Hodges' proposals, some offering ideas of their own. The need to make the Club more attractive to younger officers and thus to persuade many more to join was widely stressed – though with occasional dissent – and the opening of membership to the Nursing Service and the

WRAF advocated. Payment of subscriptions by means of block membership for officers' messes or by charging all officers a day's pay were suggested also. Some expressed regret, particularly a former Chairman who felt his share of responsibility for the failure of past Committees to grip the problem which confronted the present one. Only two speakers, on the other hand, came out strongly against the proposed Working Party, one of them – unsurprisingly – Wing Commander Reynolds, who spoke at length. Critical of the procedure being used at the meeting, he dismissed some of the suggestions being put forward and contended that the only sensible way ahead was first to 'put the house in order' and then wait for a major developer to come forward with a scheme for the whole of the Piccadilly/Park Lane corner which would entail the Club being paid a proper price for the remaining 55 years of its Lease. In the meantime, he felt, the Club had no choice but to continue its policy of increasing prices and subscriptions and asserted that Hodges' proposals would not get the Club out of its present difficulties. Hardly anyone was convinced by this and when the question was put to the vote the subscription increases were rejected by 143 votes to 4. Among those present and strongly supportive of Hodges was Sir Dermot Boyle.

Two days later the Committee reviewed what had been in effect a vote of no confidence. Reynolds, quite undaunted, thought there was nothing in what Hodges had said and it would be completely irresponsible for the Committee to change its mind. The other members, however, had no doubt, as Group Captain Richards put it, that the intention and motive behind the vote was clear and that the subscription should be held until the next AGM so as to give Hodges time to draw up his scheme. Pretty, determined to guide the discussion, stated that his contacts with serving and retired officers showed how staggered they were at the course the Committee had been steering; consequent resignations, he thought, could end up much higher than anticipated. If Hodges were to be given a chance and the Committee could hold the position for the next year or so it might be worthwhile. So by seven votes to one (Reynolds having previously left the meeting) they agreed to take up Hodges' offer. Immediately Pretty wrote to all Club members telling them that subscriptions were not now going to be raised but other charges would be, inviting them to contribute to a special Survival Fund intended to reduce the bank overdraft, and announcing the formation of Hodges' sub-committee to suggest ways and means of substantially increasing Club membership.

Within the next six weeks £4,270 was donated to the Survival Fund by 502 members.

It took the Working Party less than three months to compile their Report. Hodges himself, still serving in Paris, could not take part directly in its proceedings though he gave much moral support. It was Air Commodore Cameron – now at Cranwell – who chaired it, assisted by Group Captains Ivor Broom, Freddie Sowrey and Ronnie Webster, all of them attending the course at the nearby Imperial Defence College and being allowed to allot some of their 'study time' to the Club's affairs. Meeting frequently, often at the Club itself, they very quickly realised that the membership question they intended to address could not be treated in isolation from all the Club's other problems; its present and future image was crucial, and alternative ways of tackling its disturbing membership and financial situation must be examined. They realised too the importance of obtaining as wide a range of views as possible on the question: 'why are so few officers members of the RAF Club?' So all Commanders-in-Chief were brought into the consultations and the sub-committee members – widely known and respected in the RAF – exploited their many contacts. As a case in point, in March 1965 when word about the Club's affairs reached Group Captain Bob Freer, in Singapore as CO of Seletar and just about as far away as it was possible to get, he wrote to the Chairman giving the strongest support for drastic measures to put the Club on a sound footing, including laying an obligation on every permanent list RAF officer to be a member and pay a modest annual subscription.

Cameron, as chairman of the working party, was also able as a member of the Club Committee to keep it informed on progress and to take part in the continuing more general deliberations about the Club's survival. On 6 January 1965, for example, he faced up to Reynolds' continuing pressure for the subscription increases by stating that the working party's aim was no less than a 15,000 increase in membership, insisting that the Club would go to the wall unless the RAF took a dynamic interest in it, and urging the Committee not to 'hog-tie' them by an early announcement about raised subscriptions. On 3 February Hodges also attended in order to report progress. Their proposed scheme, he said, would centre on all serving officers, including women, paying nominal subscriptions through officers' messes; the Committee would be chaired by a serving officer, and the atmosphere would be more like a hotel than a club. Two weeks later, in the Executive Committee, Reynolds – with some support – reiterated his total opposition to Hodges' 'impracticable ideas', and his conviction that higher subscriptions, long-term redevelopment of the site, and all-male membership no higher than 2,000 was the only way forward. This was a totally different concept from the RAF-centred Club that Hodges and his allies were promoting. On 3 March, however, Cameron reported again, this time on the visits he and Hodges had paid to home Commanders-in-Chief and their letters to those overseas. These had been followed up on stations and the responses were overwhelmingly supportive. He and Hodges were now convinced the scheme would work, and they thought the RAF Central Fund might help with a grant or loan.

By now the Working Party Report was being circulated. Running to eleven pages, it summarised the Club's history and its present difficulties, pointing out that with only 8 per cent of the RAF's serving officers being members, it was far removed from Lord Cowdray's original concept. The image of the Club, the Report stated, was of a dusty, gloomy old place, full of senior and retired officers and providing nothing to attract younger ones who wanted a welcoming atmosphere in which to entertain wives or girl-friends; it was out-of-date and a stark contrast with contemporary RAF officers' messes. Nothing had been done to modernise it since most actual members appeared content with it and the management reflected their ages and attitudes. The various options that had now been considered included subscription and price increases, amalgamation with another Club (the United Services Club had made an approach on 17 February) and the closure of particular facilities. All were rejected. Site redevelopment, while attractive in some ways, would be an admission of defeat, and a straight recruiting drive would fail unless the root causes of Service disinterest were addressed. So the Working Party recommended a block mess membership scheme with a £1.10s. subscription for all serving officers regardless of rank, thus enabling a Club to be created that would act as a social club/hotel for officers and wives and a venue for a variety of Service and private functions. In other words Hodges and his team were basing their concept on what they had already observed in the Cercle Militaire in Paris (and heard about in similar clubs in Brussels and Rome), and the practical measures they went on to propose in terms of management, accommodation, prices, internal redevelopment, and the status of wives were all geared to this end.

Concluding their Report they asserted that the present-day RAF had a real responsibility to their successors to see that the Club did not go to the wall, and went on:

> We feel that the Service as a whole has never heard of Cowdray's generosity and the reason behind his original offer and this omission should be remedied. Nor does the Service fully recognise that 128 Piccadilly is a building which was bought on its behalf to be utilised as a 'permanent club home for the Service'. If this position is put fairly and frankly to the Service there will be no hesitation in their response, and we could eventually achieve a social Headquarters in London of which the RAF can be justifiably proud.

At this stage, of course, the Report was only in draft form and could not be generally circulated, so the AGM on 25 March 1965 was limited to the usual formalities, after which the Chairman invited Hodges to describe the progress his team was making (no record of his summary has been found). Soon afterwards, however, Sir Walter Pretty decided it was time to make way for a new Chairman and on 14 April the Committee not only elected Neil Cameron to succeed him but also Group Captains Broom, Sowrey and Webster to join them. So now 'the Colonels' were not just putting their ideas together but were also on the inside, charged with tackling the immediate practical problems still confronting the Club. They were immeasurably strengthened by the knowledge that their scheme was backed by the Air Force Board and by all the Commanders-in-Chief – the kind of moral support that the Club had never before been given. Yet as Cameron told his Committee on 12 May, they faced the gravest time the Club had ever experienced: it was nearly bankrupt and their decisions in the next few months would be critical.

One of the most urgent moves needed was to reopen the bid for a major grant or loan from the RAF Central Fund. Cameron had already raised the possibility in January and been turned down by the Chairman of the day. Undaunted, he had then talked with the Director General of Personal Services, Air Vice-Marshal G. T. B. Clayton, who said that the Fund's Committee was adopting a much more constructive policy under its new Chairman, the recently appointed AMP, Air Marshal Sir David Lee. Suitably encouraged, Cameron went to see Lee, who intimated that the Club would need to obtain Charitable Status if the Central Fund were to be persuaded to make a sizeable contribution to its funds. He also made it clear that the Air Force Board could not agree to the imposition of a compulsory membership scheme, which would in any case be incompatible with serving officers' subscriptions being payable through the Pay Agents in the way that officers' regular donations to the RAF Benevolent Fund had been collected since 1938. Having reported the advice about Charitable Status to the Committee on 12 May, Cameron took legal advice which suggested that if two-thirds of serving officers joined the Club the prospects were good. He next met the Deputy Commissioner for Charities, who was 'very helpful', and then went back to David Lee, to whom he suggested a grant of £80,000. Lee resigned his Club membership at this point, considering it would be improper for him to be seen as urging the cause of an organisation of which he himself was a member – he rejoined on retirement. The grant was approved by the Central Fund on 2 June, subject to registration of the Club as a charity.

When, however, Cameron explained this new prospect at a special committee meeting on 28 July, it seemed to some members that they were being railroaded down the Hodges route. Richards, Vice-Chairman and hitherto supportive, led the dissentients. He was 'not concerned with ladies, etc., but with the liquidation of the Club and turning it into a charitable institution'; it would no longer be a members' club run by the members but would pass under the control of Command Representatives and Charity Commissioners. He accused Cameron of 'trying to bulldoze Hodges' through the Committee and went so far as to threaten High Court action. Cameron's response was firm. The Board of the Central Fund – itself a charity – was very keen to help, but the purse strings could not possibly be opened to the extent necessary without the Charity Commission being persuaded that the Club was 'serving the morale of the RAF'. For most of the Committee there was no choice but to press on, but not until the end of 1966 did they win this particular battle.

Meanwhile, in mid-1965, the Committee addressed two other equally urgent tasks. One was to awaken the interest and enthusiasm of that vast majority of serving officers who had hitherto virtually ignored the Club; the other was to inform and seek the support of all the existing members. Hodges took on the first in a personal letter sent on 28 June to every one of the 20,500 RAF, PMRAFNS and WRAF officers serving at home and abroad. Sowrey still remembers seeing large quantities of these letters being loaded aboard Transport Command aircraft for despatch overseas. Summarising the Club's origins, its present-day difficulties and the new-style concept now being devised, Hodges pleaded for their support on the basis of an annual subscription of two-thirds of a day's pay being deducted at source by the paying agents. Initially, since the Club needed to measure the Service reaction to this plan, he asked for a simple form to be completed and returned via units, and promised to write again afterwards.

The second letter, from Cameron, was sent in September to all 3,489 Club members. This set the scene in more detail, reviewed the Hodges Committee's proposals, mentioned the possibilities of Charitable Status and a Central Fund grant or loan, and reported that 85 per cent of the 11,500 replies so far received to Hodges' letter were supportive. The Committee concluded that subject to the backing of 75 per cent of all serving officers the Hodges scheme provided the only practicable basis for the Club's future and recommended that members should approve it. They were asked to sign and return the enclosed form and depending on the response an Extraordinary General Meeting (EGM) would be held to amend the Club rules. All members, present or not, would be entitled to vote. Within a month 2,380 replies had been received, all but 20 in favour, and with the Committee having accepted the Hodges proposals the EGM was scheduled for 10 November.

In the meantime Cameron's 'new-look' Committee had also been turning their minds to the organisation and working of the Club. In April the old Finance and Redevelopment Sub-Committee had been superseded by a Ways and Means Committee (Sowrey, Broom and Webster) tasked to report on ways of improving the short-term finances. In May they recommended employing management consultants to examine the organisation and catering, providing additional double bedrooms, letting the basement storage space, closing the Park Lane entrance and moving the office to the front area. In June, however, the Club was still receiving enquiries from potential redevelopers and in July – despite Reynolds' recent resignation – there remained deep divisions about the direction and pace of change being insisted upon. Nevertheless, by October, his convictions much strengthened by the responses to the recent letters, Cameron brought his four henchmen (now including Wing Commander R. D. Bruce) into a 'Way Ahead Committee' chaired by Sowrey; their task was to consider the practical steps needed to create a new image for the Club. At the same time Hodges, about to return to the MOD as ACAS(Ops), was unanimously co-opted to the main Committee. So by November 1965 the new team was largely in place, important negotiations were in hand, and major changes in the Club itself were being planned. It remained to obtain the formal authority of the members, and fast, if the finances were to be rescued in time.

In his opening address to the EGM Cameron linked the struggle for the Club's survival with the wider battle still being fought to preserve the RAF itself as a separate Service, a conviction which he knew was shared by hundreds of members who had written over recent months. At the heart of the challenge, he went on, was membership. The Club had no more than 1,500 serving members – a mere 200 of them aged under 27 – and if it was to live it needed 'a health-giving transfusion of young blood'. Having then outlined the desperate state of the finances and applauded the heart-warming response to the Survival Fund, he spoke of the first-class support now being given to the Hodges Report. Some might say, he concluded, that the new Committee was trying to move too fast, but the money had been draining away and action was urgent. So he asked the meeting to authorise implementation of the Report's proposals and amendment of the Club rules to enable WRAF and Nursing Officers to become full members and to permit members' wives, as Associate Members, to use the Club without the husband being present, to bring in their children aged 14 and over, and to introduce female guests.

The ensuing questions essentially sought clarification or reassurance. One member who hoped that officers would not be press-ganged into joining was told that there was no question of this; another asked if wives would pay subscriptions, to which the answer was 'No, not at this stage.' A previous Committee member, while supportive, doubted whether the necessary number of new members would be attained and enquired about alternative plans, i.e., either redevelopment or amalgamation with another club; this gave Hodges the opportunity to review his findings and say how convinced he was that the required result would be achieved. The only other serious issue raised was whether retired members would be expected to pay more than the serving ones, and here the Chairman had to plead for more time to get such matters sorted out. The appropriate Resolution was then passed.

There followed a general discussion, during which Sowrey's 'Way Ahead Committee' was encouraged to 'let boldness be its guide' in making the Club more attractive to its younger members; the use of the hitherto empty basement to offer supper and dancing facilities was suggested; and business expertise should be brought into the management structure, possibly with a civilian manager. In response to questions the method of paying subscriptions was explained together with the hopes of acquiring Charitable Status and help from the Central Fund. One or two light-hearted reminiscences appeared too. One member referred to No 4 Park Lane having been used as a brothel and much patronised by younger officers, and another – anxious to allay members' fears about the ladies – observed that Bruton Street, the Club's first home, had been dominated by women: 'We had three ladies called Betty, Josie and Ethel, and the Club was all the better for it!'

The next day Hodges wrote again to all RAF, WRAF and Nursing Officers, reporting the most gratifying response to his earlier letter and bringing them up to date. Having listed the facilities that already existed and were now being adapted to the Club's new purposes, he invited them all to complete the enclosed 'form of authority' in order to join with effect from January 1966. Three months later Cameron was able to report to the AGM that the Service membership had mushroomed to 12,000.

Yet over the winter months, depressingly but hardly unexpectedly, the Committee had become aware of skeletons in the cupboard. Its investigations had revealed that in the recent past there had been inadequate control over general expenditure, costs and profit margins, buying and checking of purchases, and rendering and recovery of bills. There had been little or no wages and employment policy; whereas hotels, restaurants and successful Clubs paid some 25 per cent of their turnover in wages, the Club was paying 44.7 per cent – yet not enough of this was going to the good staff. Then there were dishonest office staff, failure to follow-up bills incurred by members, unpaid private function bills. Even worse the membership records were in 'complete chaos'. Among other things there were no accurate lists of non-serving members or of subscriptions, many bankers' orders were illegible, and the list of membership proposals was out of date. The clerk responsible was dismissed in January 1966 and membership cards were introduced at the end of the year. Determined not to push such matters under the carpet, Cameron described this situation to the AGM, explained the measures already in hand to rectify it, and paid tribute to the staff who had been doing the hard work. These included Squadron Leader A. J. Hayter, a serving officer on loan to the Club from the RAF to 'recover the position in the office', and the Secretary, Group Captain Rogers, a close personal friend, who had done so much for the Club but become ill through overwork. He had now retired and would soon be replaced by Mr W. A. Jolly, a former Commander in the Navy's supply branch with much subsequent experience in hotel management. Once he was installed Cameron envisaged the Club being run by a small Executive Committee consisting of serving, retired and non-serving officers and meeting monthly, together with a General Committee meeting quarterly and acting virtually as a board of governors. This would be twice the size and include representatives nominated by Commanders-in-Chief.

Cameron now turned to the finances. These did not present a very joyful picture, with the overdraft at a record figure of £57,900 and a working loss of £15,900, but he remained optimistic about the increased income that would now accrue from the Hodges scheme. He was very hopeful, too, of supplementing this with a grant and a loan from the Central Fund totalling £90,000. Soon, therefore, it should be possible to start the modernisation of the Club, with priority being given to installing oil-fired central heating, improving the plumbing, developing the fourth-floor bedrooms, and cleaning the whole place up; the Club was dirty, in need of redecoration and re-carpeting, and the kitchens in particular were deplorable. It would need every penny it could get. In the subsequent discussion Cameron and his colleagues received strong support. Among other things he assured members that the Bank was firmly behind their efforts, that better supervision of the staff and improved pay for 'the good and faithful' were high on the agenda, and that the Club was keen to encourage extensive use of its facilities by members' wives, all of whom would be Associate Members and not required to pay separate subscriptions.

Meanwhile the Committee had been tackling other important matters. One was the Lease Redemption Policy, currently valued at £21,700, intended to reach £25,000 in 2019* and costing £1,750 per annum. The Club would do better, it was decided, to cancel the policy and invest the capital in the stock market – a move which initially yielded £23,500 and was eventually to prove eminently sound. Another even more significant subject was the almost interminable debate about Charitable Status. Its implications had been first spelt out in October 1965, when the Club was

---

* Throughout this period the date for the expiry of the Lease was regularly and mistakenly quoted in Committee as 2015 instead of 2019.

told that Trustees would have to be appointed who would be enabled through the Committee to run the Club, but not allowed to spend or deal with its capital without the Charity Commissioners' permission; in other words sale or redevelopment of 128 Piccadilly would require their agreement. Now confident of success, Cameron still realised that the process might take some time, so he and Hodges decided to go ahead with the formal request to AMP (Lee) for financial support. The request was lodged in April 1966 and on 2 June the Central Fund approved a provisional grant of £80,000. At this point another obstacle emerged when the Inland Revenue showed signs of objecting to the grant of Charitable Status. The Charity Commissioners then declared themselves prepared to mount a legal challenge if necessary and advised the Air Ministry to tell the Club to adopt the necessary draft Memorandum of Association. This would need to specify the hand-over of the Club's assets to RAF charities should it ever close; the Club would also agree that the money would be spent on essential improvements and maintenance and accounted for to the Central Fund.

It remained to put the Memorandum of Association and the necessary Rule changes to the membership and on 10 November 1966 Cameron proposed the appropriate Resolution to a packed Extraordinary General Meeting. The Central Fund, he said, had displayed some symptoms of shock at the size of the grant being requested, but on the whole had taken it well; they could not, however, authorise a penny piece unless the Club became a charity. The Memorandum of Association was drafted to provide that:

1. It was to be a proprietary club rather than a members' club.
2. The RAF Club Company (p. 14) would be the proprietors, with three Directors and a Secretary. Sir Dermot Boyle, Air-Vice Marshal Hodges and Air Commodore Cameron (as Club Chairman) would be the Directors, with the General Manager as Secretary.
3. Its objects would be:
   a. to promote the efficiency of the RAF by fostering the esprit de corps of RAF officers.
   b. to provide a residential Club in London at affordable prices.
   c. to encourage an interest in flying, particularly in the RAF.
   d. to encourage Service reunions and provide a venue for the entertainment of representatives of foreign air forces.
   e. to encourage serving officers to meet with retired officers and benefit from their knowledge and experience.

4. It would be non-profit-making.
5. Wives of members would be Associate Members.

The Charity Commissioners too had been extremely helpful, and acting on their advice the Committee had drafted various alterations now needed in the Club's Rules. These changes now required approval, together with the draft Memorandum of Association (see above). Given acceptance of the Resolution by a two-thirds majority (he hoped it would be unanimous) Cameron would write next day to the Central Fund requesting the cheque for the £80,000 so urgently needed to enable the development programme to start.

If Cameron expected an easy passage he was to be disappointed, for he now had to listen to a statement lasting almost 30 minutes from Wing Commander Reynolds. Having mentioned the disagreement with the Hodges scheme which had led to his earlier resignation from the Committee, he subjected the text of the proposals to detailed and critical examination in an attempt to warn his audience of the dangers they could be running through in effect losing control of their Club. He went so far as to ask what would happen if the Club failed financially or, even worse, the RAF ceased to exist – an argument hardly likely to impress the Chairman as one of the strongest believers in the independent Service! Since members had been given virtually no advance notice of the proposals, he requested a 28-day adjournment of the meeting to enable them to be independently studied. One or two further speakers shared to some extent Reynolds' concerns, expressing doubts about the validity of the financial projections and wondering what would happen if in a few years' time the Charity Commissioners were to say 'Close'. Most, however, accepted the Chairman's assertion that the whole situation had been very carefully considered and agreed that there was in fact no alternative; even so there was still some support for a short delay. A brief Committee discussion ensued, after which – the Chairman having refused to accept an amendment – the Resolution was put to the vote and carried on a show of hands.

Now, with the tension eased, Cameron gave details of various changes already under way. The Sinking Fund had been reorganised to bring in £300,000 in 2019, the Staff Benevolent Fund was being rearranged and the wages of 'our best and most faithful employees' had been brought into line with rates elsewhere. Oil-fired central heating had been installed and radiators were to be put in all bedrooms (some of which still had no heating at all), and nine bedrooms had been modernised. Moreover a modern machine-accounting system had been introduced so that the General Manager now knew on a day-to-day basis what was going on. Then there was the promised 'New Look'. The Dining Room service ('pathetic', Cameron called it) would be quickly tackled. 'The much under-used and beautiful smoke room' would become the main mixed bar overlooking Green Park. The bar and cafeteria on the ground floor would be turned into a 'very nice, leather-bound smoke room' for men only. The mixed bar (today's Victoria Bar) would be converted to a writing room and tea room, and the Ballroom ('it looks terrible') redecorated. The big development, he concluded, was to be in the basement – at present full of rubbish – where there was ample space for a bar, a Buttery luncheon service and a small dance floor. There would even be room for a swimming pool should funds become available.

The Chairman concluded by paying tribute to the 19 Committee members, several of long standing, who had accepted the new concept and worked tremendously hard to get it going. Some with other major commitments would now be departing, including Air Vice-Marshal Hodges, and soon afterwards Cameron himself was to be drawn away elsewhere and succeeded as Chairman by Air Commodore Freddie Sowrey. The President too was shortly to change, when following the death of Sir John Salmond on 16 April 1968, Sir Dermot Boyle readily accepted the Committee's warm invitation to succeed him.

CHAPTER 8

NEW CHALLENGES

W as it just coincidence that the greatest turning-point in the Club's history occurred at a time when the RAF itself was facing one of its most significant revolutions? The post-war years had thus far seen the continuance of world-wide roles which stretched back into the pre-war era; the structure of the Service still reflected that of the 1930s; there had been a whole series of limited war operations conducted in cooperation with the Royal Navy and the Army, depending on far-flung bases and air mobility, and culminating in the recent Confrontation with Indonesia. True there had been major changes, most notably the advent of the jet age, the development of NATO, and the creation of the UK's nuclear deterrent. But there remained a 'traditional look' about many aspects of the Service and its responsibilities. Now, however, it was becoming recognised – not least by the politicians – that the Armed Services could no longer attempt to do a bit of everything and that the Defence Vote would have to be concentrated on the NATO theatre and the Cold War, with forces based essentially at home and in Central and Southern Europe. The RAF's emphasis would also need to switch to smaller numbers of newer types of aircraft, employing the rapidly advancing technologies and relying on increased levels of expertise and professionalism at all levels.

So the late 1960s and early 1970s witnessed a series of wide-ranging defence reviews, withdrawals from East of Suez, and – with much else – dramatic reductions in RAF officer strength. Not surprisingly the RAF's leaders, much concerned about preserving morale, now recognised – unlike in earlier years – the significance of the Club in helping to bind together the officer corps of which some 75 per cent were members. Virtually all the top brass themselves belonged, they were kept informed and being consulted about the Club's activities and plans, they were lending their support to active measures to hold the membership firm and encourage newly commissioned officers to join. The 'Colonels' Revolt' had in fact put the new Club structure in place at precisely the right time. Without it the Club would probably have failed to meet the challenges of a new era in the RAF's history; with it the Club was able not just to survive but to exploit the changing circumstances of the 1970s. The rapidly mounting inflation of these years would almost inevitably have wrecked the 'old-look' Club, whereas the far greater number of serving members – all subscribing a fixed percentage of their steadily increasing salaries (see p. 104) – enabled the Club's most important single source of income to keep pace. Indeed it did more, permitting the much needed development programme to be successfully funded under the direction of an increasingly professional Committee and effective management.

At the top of the tree (see Appendix A) was the President. In May 1967 Neil Cameron had invited the Committee's view on the election procedure and elicited the general opinion that the incumbent should be a Senior Officer 'as being in keeping with the new outlook and close association with the Service'. Sir Dermot Boyle was accordingly elected and 12 years later his retirement was suitably recorded by the Committee, at that time chaired by Air Commodore Robin Lees (whose father had also been Chairman):

> He has maintained a close interest in the affairs of the Club, encouraging and guiding successive Chairmen with that unfailing sense of humour, common sense and good fellowship for which he is so well-known ... he gave the staunchest support for the revitalisation of the Club in 1966.

Boyle was then invited, with the approval of Her Majesty the Queen as Patron, to become the Club's first Vice-Patron – a position which had existed since the earliest years of the Club but never been filled.

His successor, who had eventually become MRAF the Lord Cameron of Balhousie, sadly died in office in 1985; recording his death the Club Newsletter recalled his prominent role in the revitalisation of the Club in the 1960s, and the way in which his guiding hand had since rested firmly and unobtrusively on the helm. Another former 'Colonel' took his place in 1986, Air Chief Marshal Sir Lewis Hodges; he had already spent 26 years as a Director of the RAF Club Company and when he relinquished the Presidency in 1993 was described as a great friend of the Club who in the difficult mid-1960s had piloted it through very turbulent waters. It was without doubt very much due to his foresight and endeavours that the Club today was such a thriving organisation.

Subsequently MRAF Sir Michael Beetham, a long-serving former CAS, filled the post for ten years, always taking the closest interest in the Club's affairs and making many valuable suggestions for improvement to its facilities. Then in 2002 MRAF the Lord Craig of Radley took over, having earlier served both as CAS and as Chief of the Defence Staff. As well as the painting of Lord Cowdray, portraits of all the RAF officers who became Presidents hang in the Club, four of them in the Presidents' Room (see pp. 129–30).

Since 1967 there have also been at any one time up to twelve Vice-Presidents, most of them serving officers holding executive positions on the Air Force Board or as Commanders-in-Chief, and the rest continuing in office on retirement – either, as former Chiefs of Air Staff, for life, or for two or three more years before making way for others. The rationale underlying this system, as introduced by Cameron, was to try to preserve the recently established links with the RAF's leaders, and the annual briefing and formal dinner for the Vice-Presidents instituted in 1968 has continued ever since. In 1981 the Chairman (still Robin Lees) defined the Committee policy on selection: they would be chosen from senior officers whose appointments would enable them to use their influence for the Club's benefit, and the honour being bestowed upon them would take account of their length of membership and previous interest in Club affairs. Theirs has never been a formal role in the Club's management, but on many occasions, especially on controversial issues, the Committee has greatly welcomed their counsel. This has been a major factor in preserving the ties with the RAF which were established by the 'Colonels' and remain just as important today.

The single most important appointment has, of course, been that of Chairman. Strangely perhaps, the appointment procedure seems never to have been clearly defined. The Club's constitution lays down that he shall be elected at the AGM, but while this happens as a formality it is not based on an open nomination procedure. Rarely has there even been recorded Committee discussion. The key to the system seems to lie in Air Commodore Sowrey's suggestion to the Committee in November 1967 that he should approach the Air Secretary's Branch for a possible successor. The Committee agreed and in due course Air Commodore Basil Hamilton's name went forward to the next AGM. Not until 1982 did this subject appear again in the minutes, when Robin Lees recommended Air Commodore Geoff Claridge to be his successor, 'as he was the Service choice'. Next time round 'The President and Senior Officers' were recorded as recommending Air Commodore Robert Wood. The pattern of Chairmen up to the early 1990s indicates that all but two held the post for one tour of RAF duty in or near the MOD (Robin Lees and Robert Wood each served two such tours) and the choice was probably made by the Air Secretary's Department in consultation with CAS and the President. So Cameron and later Hodges doubtless had their say as well. By the 1990s, however, there remained so few suitable RAF appointments in the London area that there was hardly any choice. So in 1996 the Committee accepted the Chairman's view that the only serving air officer in the London area whose job would from now on allow him the necessary time was the Senior Directing Staff (Air) at the nearby Royal College of Defence Studies. Nowadays, therefore, with the blessing of CAS and the President, the incumbent – a Club member of course – serves as Chairman.

If this may seem an unusual arrangement it must be remembered that the Club is a proprietary, not a members' club (see p. 90), with Charitable Status and a charter which ties it closely to the interests of the Service.* Its recovery and continuing progress since the late 1960s provide clear evidence of the quality and hard work of the successive Chairmen (see Appendix A) whose time has been made available to it by the RAF; their leadership and ability to cope with challenges of many kinds have been of inestimable value. If at times it has seemed that the Club could have benefited from less frequent changes in the chairmanship, it is the Vice-Chairmen who have provided much-needed continuity. Over the whole period there have been but four: Harry Summers, John Briggs, Leonard Williams and Geoff Claridge. All have been retired officers, bringing with them invaluable experience of the outside business world as well as knowledge of the Club, and all serving long enough to proffer much-needed guidance and assistance. The current Vice-Chairman, Air Commodore Geoff Claridge, is himself a former Chairman who has devoted himself unstintingly to the Club's affairs since November 1994.

A few of the General and Executive Committee members, too, have served for many years, including some who first joined the Committee as serving officers when nominated as Command, Group or Station Representatives. They have brought special skills and experience to the Club's affairs. The majority of Committee members, however, have served for relatively short periods, most of them representing the present-day RAF and bringing to their appointments a mix of genuine enthusiasm and up-to-date knowledge.

* Plans are presently afoot to convert the Club to a Company Limited by Guarantee.

Bust of Air Commodore Sir Frank
Whittle, by James Butler

Bust of Sir Barnes Wallis,
by Marcus Kaye

Bust of R. J. Mitchell,
by James Butler

Bust of Roy Chadwick,
by James Butler

Above left: Marshal of the Royal Air Force Sir John Salmond, by Cuthbert J. Orde
Above right: Marshal of the Royal Air Force The Lord Craig of Radley, by Richard Smyly
Below left: Marshal of the Royal Air Force Sir Dermot Boyle, by Carlos Sancha
Below right: Marshal of the Royal Air Force Sir Michael Beetham, by John Walton

Air Chief Marshal Sir Lewis
Hodges, by Leonard Boden

Marshal of the Royal Air Force
The Lord Cameron of Balhousie,
by Norman Hepple

Above: Berlin Airlift, by Michael Turner. Below: Ponies on the Moor, by Frank Wootton

Above: Vulcan Scramble, by Frank Wootton
Below: Black Buck One, by Keith Woodcock

Tornado over Urquhart Castle, by Ronald Wong

Harriers 'in the field', by Stuart Brown

No 208 Squadron Buccaneers, by Michael Rondot

The Smoking
Room in the 1950s

The Club
Lounge in 1967

The Cowdray
Room in 2004

A bedroom in the 1960s

A bedroom in 2004

The Dining Room in 2004

The Club has benefited also from the increased continuity and professionalism of its Secretaries. Indeed since Mr Jolly resigned in 1968 in order to become Secretary of the Carlton Club there have been only three. Mr Edward Jeffreys, already experienced elsewhere as a Club Secretary, held the post until 1975 when he received a small pension and moved on to the Lansdowne Club. The Committee now decided to combine the duties with those of General Manager and their searches led to the appointment of Squadron Leader James Swaffield, who in 1966 had retired early from the RAF Catering Branch for family reasons. Having previously completed a two-year part-time course leading to a Diploma in Management Studies, he then joined Forte and Company. Here, after filling a succession of managerial posts, he became Director of the Airports Division on the Board of Trust House Forte Airport Services Ltd. Now a Fellow of the Hotel and Catering Industry Management Association (FHCIMA), he brought to the Club a much firmer management style – and of course RAF experience. Over the next 15 years he oversaw many of the improvements in its structure that will be described in Chapters 9 and 10. He was succeeded in 1991 by Mr Peter Owen, another FHCIMA. Selected from 140 applicants, six of them short-listed, he already had 23 years' experience in the hotel and catering industry both at home and overseas – most recently in Sweden – and was ideally qualified to continue his predecessor's work of moving the Club into the computer age and to develop the most modern management techniques. The one gap in his qualifications, i.e., knowledge of the RAF, was quickly rectified when he was sent on a number of familiarisation visits to Headquarters and stations, and he remains the key and greatly respected figure in the whole direction of the Club.

Ever since the 1960s' revolution the size and shape of the membership has remained of prime concern to the Committee. The initial challenge, however, was very different from earlier days; it was the risk of overcrowding. In 1967, such was the greatly increased usage by serving members that efforts to recruit more retired officers were quietly put on hold. In 1968 measures were actually discussed to restrict non-serving membership, and in 1970 it was announced that a waiting-list might need to be introduced. In the event only one restriction was ever imposed, i.e., in 1968 when Volunteer Reserve (Training) officers were ruled as ineligible. Two years later, after protests from on high, Air Commodore Colin Kunkler, who would go on to serve the Committee for many years, studied the arguments and persuaded his colleagues to withdraw the rule.

It was at this time (1972) that the Club's serving membership reached its all-time high: 15,572, which with the steadily rising numbers of non-serving members enabled it to pass the magic grand total of 20,000. This then dipped for a few years before eventually reaching its all-time record of 21,717 in 1991. During these twenty years, however, the serving membership had fallen by one-third in the 1970s, reflecting the sharp decline in the size of the officer corps, and steadily but much more slowly in the 1980s. Counter-balancing these losses were the retired members, whose strength doubled so that in 1991 they comprised some 55 per cent of the total.

The decline in serving membership in the 1970s and 1980s had been watched with some anxiety by the Committee. Recognising that much of it was inevitably being caused by the contraction of the RAF, they also saw a fall in the percentage of serving officers who were actually members. In the mid-1970s this averaged nearly 77 per cent; in the early 1980s it fell sharply to around 66 per cent. In the short term this did not affect the Club's well-being since the number of retired members continued to rise steadily, but the longer-term prospect was worrying because the Club would eventually have a decreasing number of eligible members on whom to draw. So 1981 witnessed the first of various campaigns to attract more serving officers, and especially among those newly commissioned. Improved publicity material including new brochures and videos was circulated; Command, Group and Station representatives were suitably briefed at the Club and charged with publicising its facilities within their units; the Vice-Presidents' active support was obtained; and special efforts were directed at Cranwell, where initial officer training was coming to be concentrated. At times the Cranwell staff were able to arrange for the cadets to spend a day at the Club and numerous applications for membership usually resulted. Sadly, however, cost and shortage of syllabus time all too often precluded such visits. So at the end of the 1980s all the Committee's efforts were doing no more than maintain the overall Service membership at a disappointing 65 per cent of the officer corps.

Partly thanks to the rule change of 1966, several hundred Nursing and WRAF officers had also been contributing to the membership, and from 1969 widows whose husbands had died over the age of 65 were allowed to become full members in their own names. Nevertheless there remained one potentially divisive issue. While most of the public rooms were open to members of both sexes, the men retained sole use of the Gentlemen's Bar and therefore the Smoking Room to which it gave access. Until 1987 this limitation had been uncontroversial; indeed most London Clubs maintained far more restrictive policies towards lady members and visitors. Now, however, the General Committee decreed that the Smoking Room should be available to all, so that ladies as well as gentlemen could be encouraged to use it for the sort of informal business discussions that were thought inappropriate in other public areas of the Club. So on 23 December a notice was posted announcing the intention to re-name the rooms as the Writing Room and the Members' Bar; while it was not thought that members would have valid reasons to oppose these changes, written objections would be considered.

The reaction took the Committee totally by surprise. At lunch time on 13 January 1988 some 20 retired members, all regular users of the Gentlemen's Bar, gathered at the urging of Squadron Leader Harris, affectionately nicknamed 'Bomber', to seek support for a resolution to retain the status quo ante. Also encouraged by Harris to come along to the Club were reporters and photographers from the *Daily Telegraph* and several other national newspapers, all of which ran the story together with radio and television. The 70-year-old wartime Liberator pilot (no relation of Sir Arthur) was reported as 'scrambling the Few' in 'the Club's 1940', with Air Commodore Richard Kyle, the Club Chairman, uncomfortably cast as the enemy. Out of the blue a seemingly innocuous change had become an issue between the male chauvinists and the supporters of women's rights. The immediate result was a paper signed by 37 members requesting an Emergency General Meeting.

This EGM took place on 22 February, when the 150 members attending heard the Chairman explain that the Committee's essential purpose was to make greater use of the little-used Smoking Room; it was thought unlikely that many ladies would wish to use the Bar except as a route to it. Strong views were expressed in the ensuing debate. Harris's 'old guard' were firm in their determination to preserve the traditions and character of the Club, which must continue to provide 'somewhere to chat without the good ladies', as applied in most other London Clubs. Few wives wanted to use either room, they contended, and the Committee should be able to find somewhere else for them. Countering these views were senior Committee members, others from the older generation, and younger officers, who saw no logic in WRAF officers, as full members, being discriminated against. One of the ladies present challenged the comment and spoke of feeling insulted by some of the views expressed; the present regulations were inequitable and 'we ladies should ask politely for the Club's full facilities'. Committee members observed that the tide towards change was unstoppable and urged the meeting to remember the great assistance the Club received from the RAF, which itself pursued an equal opportunities policy. There was no choice, they said, but to give lady members similar recognition. Several members, persuaded by such arguments, thought that a vote should take place throughout the Club and not just in a 'packed meeting'. Nevertheless the old guard won the day by the narrowest margin: 74 votes to 71.

Disinclined to leave the matter there, the Committee now took up the suggestion of a postal ballot on the principle of keeping the men-only bar, and on a vote of almost 9,000 some 60 per cent declared themselves against it, a result which was announced and accepted at the AGM on 4 May. The Committee nevertheless came in for considerable criticism for mishandling this particular question, but many members were also at pains to record their praise for the Committee's excellent achievements over many years in producing a first-class Club from the ashes of the 1950s. A year later, after brief discussion, during which just one member resurrected the original objections, the Gentlemen's Bar died the death.

By the early 1990s it was becoming clear that the high levels of total membership on which the Club's viability depended could not last indefinitely. Serving membership would go on falling in line with the contraction of the RAF, and retired membership – still drawn largely from the much larger officer strength of the wartime and early post-war years – was bound to start dropping soon. So in May 1991 a Membership Sub-Committee was established to examine the issues and promote a membership drive. It was asked to address a variety of questions. What could be done, for example, to answer the frequently heard criticism that the Club was for retired officers? How could officers who were not members be persuaded to join? How could the Club's attractions be better identified? How could the facilities for spouses be improved? Various measures were soon identified, most of them similar to those pursued in earlier campaigns, but also two new ones: relaxation of the regulations governing dress, and provision for under-fives. Both 'family friendly' ideas were quickly introduced, and the Sub-Committee, chaired by Carolyn Browning, has continued to monitor membership matters ever since.

Then in 1993, reacting to the latest Defence Review 'Options for Change', the Committee heard the accurate prediction that serving membership would probably drop from 9,500 to 7,500 over the next five years. This led to a proposal to create a new category of Affiliate Membership designed to cater for civilians of officer status working in general aviation or with the RAF (many of the latter might now be filling posts formerly held by officers). While this would be a radical change, one which might have implications for Charitable Status, it was agreed to investigate it. The Vice-Presidents were duly consulted, the number of such members who could be elected initially was restricted to 200, and on 4 May 1995 the scheme was put to the AGM.

It ran into fierce opposition centred on the conviction that the ethos of the Club depended upon the fact that all its members were connected with the flying services, and were serving or had served in uniform. Moreover, admission of 200 Affiliates would make little difference to the finances but could eventually prove the thin end of the wedge. Committee members strongly argued the case, with the Chairman, Air Vice-Marshal Peter Dodworth, giving examples of the sort of people they had in mind, but with 26 of the 67 votes cast going against the motion the necessary 66 per cent majority was not quite achieved. To make matters worse it later transpired that a number of station representatives who had voted against were not even Club members.

Now it was back to the drawing-board, but amid continuing anxiety about the future membership situation the Affiliate scheme was quickly reinstated in the list of desirable measures; the Club was constantly receiving requests from or on behalf of good people who were actively helping the RAF and would be assets to the Club. The arguments were well set out to members in the 1996 Newsletter as one of a series of fresh ideas being considered by a new 'Way Ahead Group' being chaired by the Vice-Chairman, and the Charity Commissioners were asked to advise on the legalities. So when the scheme came back to the members at the 1997 AGM the Chairman was able to say that most members had expressed themselves in favour; moreover Charitable Status would not be affected provided that Affiliates comprised no more than 5 per cent of the total membership and were thoroughly vetted. They must have held or be holding appropriate appointments with RAF connections, or be contributing to fulfilling the Club's objectives as defined in relation to its Charitable Status.

The ensuing discussion was in stark contrast to that of 1995. There was not one outright objector and the support was accompanied by other suggestions, including family membership. The Chairman promised to examine this idea, but in 1999 the Charity Commission effectively ruled that family membership was not within the scope of the Club's Articles. Thus far the Affiliate scheme has brought in some 200 people who meet the criteria laid down and have since been making valuable contributions to Club life. In parallel a special campaign began in 1997 to encourage more officers of the Volunteer Reserve (Training) and the Royal Auxiliary Air Force to join the Club and some 500 of them have so far responded to the appeals. Then, in 2000 following representations from the Chairman, Air-Vice Marshal Keith Filbey, the annual Cranwell visit was reinstated, leading to considerable improvement in Service membership.

So we come to today. The number of subscribing members still greatly exceeds that of most other London Clubs, and at the heart are the 7,000 serving RAF officers who include the ladies and comprise nearly 70 per cent of the total officer corps. All subscribe half a day's pay per annum. Five hundred reserve officers pay on a similar basis. The largest category are the former-serving members, who include, perhaps paradoxically, a good many serving as well as retired officers of the USAF and numerous other friendly forces. All pay annual subscriptions at rates equivalent to those applying to serving group captains. In recognition of the financial pressures faced by many such members in their later years, those of long-standing often elect to have their subscriptions frozen at the age of 65. The Club goes further for those who have completed half-centuries of unbroken membership by conferring honorary status and thus relieving them of further payments. So of the 11,000 'former-serving members' about 10,000 actually pay. These include 1,000 or more widows who chose to continue their late husbands' subscriptions (see pp. 98–9). Then there are the 200 or so Affiliates, who pay on the same basis. Finally come the 10,000 spouses of full members, who as Associate Members do not themselves subscribe but do bring much additional business to the Club. The grand total therefore lies in the region of 28,000, of whom 17,000 collectively provide the Club with a core element of its income.

CHAPTER 9

FINANCE AND FABRIC

Notwithstanding the success of the Colonels' Revolt, the Club's officials still had to face many other problems in the years that immediately followed it. At the top of the priority list, as promised in the 1966 Newsletter, was the commitment to extending the Club's amenities, and in April 1968 the Club's architect, Mr Webber, presented the Committee with a five-phase Three Year Plan, costed altogether at some £100,000. The initial phase would entail the construction of a fifth floor on the roof of the building; this would provide new staff quarters and release the whole of the fourth floor for additional members' bedrooms. Next would come extensions to the Dining Room and reorganisation of the kitchen areas, followed by alterations to the cloakrooms and then conversion of the Ladies' Lounge and Bar on the first floor to dining areas. Finally a swimming pool and sauna were proposed for the basement, together with a snack bar. Agreeing to the scheme in principle, the Committee accepted Freddie Sowrey's advice that since the Central Fund was unlikely to fund the whole scheme it should initially be asked to cover just Phase 1. So in 1969, paid for by a £25,000 loan, this work went ahead and a year later the fifth floor staff area was complete and the fourth floor entirely refurbished. The Club now possessed 21 double and 50 single rooms.

Thanks to pressures elsewhere it was a different story for the rest of the plan, most of which had to be put on hold in 1969 to enable the Committee to concentrate on raising general standards throughout the Club. In 1971, however, the development programme was resumed, this time financed by overdraft, to enable 19 single rooms to be refurbished, the TV room to be converted to a second lounge and the kitchens to be modernised. On the other hand, the proposed swimming pool was consigned to the rubbish pile; experience elsewhere, notably at the Royal Automobile Club, had shown that the capital and running costs were likely to be prohibitive, and in 1972 it was decided 'not to proceed for the time being'. However, the less ambitious disco scheme, intended to attract the younger members, had gone ahead in September 1968. This was located first in the former Ladies' Bar, re-styled in Victorian décor, and in 1970 transferred to a purpose-built room in the basement. By

1974, however, it was losing most of its appeal (see Chapter 10) and the room was transformed into a snack bar.

The mid-1970s were in fact to prove a turning-point in the Club's overall financial situation. The various improvements in its facilities in the previous few years had been almost entirely financed by loans, but from its own resources it had been unable to afford to do much more than cover its many running costs. In the late 1960s catering costs had been a particular source of anxiety, thanks largely to rising food prices and increased staff wages. Fortunately, thanks to the Club's popularity, bar profits usually offset the catering losses, though it was still judged necessary to raise food and function charges fairly frequently. The Club was, of course, sharing the consequences of the nation's increasingly parlous economic position, and in October 1971 the Committee Minutes recorded the first direct reference to 'the present inflationary situation'. In March 1974 there were stronger words. Inflation was 'in re-heat', with the official food index up by 19 per cent over the year and salaries and wages rising, so price increases for rooms and food were necessary. A year later inflation was reported up still further, at 25 per cent!

Yet the Secretary was now able to state that a considerable improvement in trading was rendering previously foreseen savings unnecessary and in the March 1975 Newsletter the Chairman, Air Vice-Marshal Ross Harding, wrote in optimistic mood about the value in these difficult times of the Club's greatest asset: its membership, with the subscription income it yielded. Four years previously the introduction of the Military Salary had prompted a review of serving members' subscriptions and the rate originally set in 1966 (p. 86) had been reduced from two-thirds to half a day's pay. Yet now, said Harding, whereas some other London Clubs were feeling the pinch of inflation severely and struggling to survive, the RAF Club's membership was holding at around 21,000 and it had just had a remarkably good year financially. Harding's successor, Air Commodore John Langston, reported in similar vein in 1977: 'amid the economic gloom which shrouded the demise of three more famous Clubs, I am delighted to report that overall we have had a very successful year'. In 1978 it was Robin Lees who explained to members the recent dramatic improvement in the Club's financial situation. Not only was there now a steadily growing surplus of income over expenditure, but the Club was also moving into net profit. This situation was being achieved mainly by greater control over staff and material costs, together with thriving use of the Club, evidenced by 80 per cent bedroom occupancy and the serving of more than 100,000 meals per year, many deriving from profitable functions.

Helping to make possible this steady transformation were significant advances in data recording and their application to the Club's activities. James Swaffield remembers that when he became Secretary in 1975 the records of non-serving members, including details of their subscriptions, were still kept on cards in box files – not all that much advanced from the 'complete chaos' of ten years before (p. 88). Fortunately, Swaffield explains, a solution was now available in the smaller computer systems now being marketed at affordable prices; one of these was installed in the General Office and the long task of transferring members' details began. The results were most satisfactory, particularly in the chasing-up and collecting of overdue subscriptions. Subsequently a much more versatile system was acquired, with a faster operating speed, additional functions and multi-terminals. The serving members were then entered in the database, making possible mass production of address labels for the annual Newsletter and also of plastic membership cards. Paid-up members could now be identified when entering the Club and those producing old, well-worn, cardboard ones were escorted to the Office where their circumstances would be investigated and they were able to reinstate their membership by paying their arrears.

The new system was also applied to functions bookings and room reservations and proved of enormous value in the Club Reception, which had hitherto relied on manual systems with all their errors and consequent underbooking. In reviewing these and other advances made possible by the advent of the early computers, not least in financial control, Swaffield remembers the enormous encouragement and support he received from his early Chairmen, John Langston and Robin Lees. He also pays special tribute to the work of Monty Lyons who ran the General Office throughout his time and whose good manners and charm are still recalled by many of the Club's longer-serving members.

Better staff management went along with all this. A major and much-needed improvement had begun in 1968 when a pension scheme was commenced with Swiss Life at a cost to the Club of £3,000 per annum. In 1975 the new scheme came into effect, bringing the Club into line with the new Social Security Act; under this 17 staff would be covered, together with the nine existing pensioners, and 18 staff too old to enter the scheme were to be paid at the same rate. Accommodation was another important staff matter that worried the Secretary. In 1971, when Jeffreys was finding difficulties in recruiting and retaining catering staff, he asked if a house could be purchased which could provide for up to 20 such employees at affordable rents. While this idea got no further, similar problems were soon affecting other groups of staff, such as valets, hall porters and receptionists, and the 1974 Newsletter also underlined the combined impact of galloping inflation and fierce competition from the London hotel industry. Clearly wage rates were too low and after an initial increase of 8 per cent a further 7.5 per cent was authorised in 1975. With the advent of the pension scheme at the same time, it was recorded that the staff on the whole appeared happy, 'being treated more in a family manner than in the big hotels and tending to stay longer in the Club's service'.

Soon afterwards it was agreed to fund yet another increase by raising catering and bar tariffs, the functions service charge, and accommodation rates, and a health insurance scheme was introduced for the senior managers. The year 1978 was marked by a 25 per cent increase in the Christmas Bonus and a one-off bonus of two-weeks' pay for all staff with a year's service or more. These were made possible by the very good trading figures which in turn had relied heavily on the staunch support of the staff themselves at a time when Club refurbishment was rendering working conditions particularly difficult. The Committee went further in 1979 by levying a 10 per cent charge on the Dining Room, Buttery and bedrooms and 12.5 per cent on functions, the entire proceeds to go to the staff as part of their guaranteed wage. The Club was recognising too the special contributions of its longest-serving members of staff, among them John Bull who had come to the Club as a page-boy in 1930, risen to be Senior Valet, and retired in 1979. 'Members will certainly miss Bull's friendly chats and personal attention ... his departure marks the passing of an era', recorded the 1980 Newsletter. Robin Lees commented in the subsequent edition on the overall staff situation. The turnover had become less disturbing, enabling the Club to be more selective in recruiting new members of management staff. The aim, he went on, was to maintain a team with both quality and experience, while competing in the wider hotel and catering world for the better professionals who were needed. Lees' successor, Geoff Claridge, was able to reinforce these measures when arranging for the Christmas Bonus to be so determined in future as to reflect the Club's profitability and the staff's contribution to it, and in 1984 a salary and wages review concentrated on the need to retain good staff in face of stiff competition. Now that revenues were available to ensure that the Club's human assets matched the much improved décor and maintenance, a 16 per cent increase was agreed overall, with 20 per cent or even more for some.

The Club's increasingly healthy financial position in the late 1970s and early 1980s also made possible much further refurbishment and redevelopment. In January 1976, the new Chairman (John Langston) accompanied Swaffield and the Vice-Chairman (Group Captain Harry Summers) on a complete inspection of the building, when it became clear just how much work was needed and the likely cost. Priorities were quickly drawn up, with new lifts and conversion of the boilers to burn gas as the most urgent, but modernisation of all the bedrooms as the most critical to the Club's image and well-being. So a costly bedroom refurbishment programme came to dominate the next few years. The plan was drawn up in 1978, when the RAF Central Fund agreed to an interest-free loan of £169,000 to cover the resultant excess of expenditure over income; it all had to be repaid within six years. Despite steadily increasing costs, averaging some 10 per cent per annum, the work went more quickly than expected, only five rooms were out of commission at any one time, and by March 1981, at a total cost of £400,000, the Club had 85 modern rooms, 53 of them singles, 32 doubles, and all fitted with radio and colour TV. It was an immense improvement, one which had uncovered many structural defects all of which had been corrected: damp walls, broken window frames, inefficient heating and so on. In a huge area of the Club the modern décor no longer cloaked more serious problems behind the façade.

Throughout this period much else was being done. In 1977 there emerged a proposal to spend £25,000 for altering the basement snack bar to provide an Old English Pub atmosphere which should be popular with younger members and also attract drinkers from the Cowdray Room. Given the identity of the public house which had originally stood on the site, there could only be one appropriate name for this new Club facility. So Air Commodore Colin Kunkler, its leading proponent, promptly wrote a brief note about 'The Running Horse Tavern' (see p. 14) for display alongside the three pewter tankards which had been recovered when the modern building was being excavated. Then came several refurbish-ments. In 1979, £50,000 was authorised for renovation of the Gentlemen's Bar and Smoking Room, quickly followed by £9,000 for improvements in the Cowdray Room. In 1981 the Lantern above the First Floor Landing was restored at a cost of £6,000; this was subsequently confirmed by the Department of Historic Buildings to be an item of historic interest. The sum of £36,000 was spent on refurbishing the Gentlemen's Cloakroom and Lavatories, and £12,000 on redecorating the Ballroom and Dining Room. In 1982, £23,000 was devoted to fitting automatic entrance doors and modernising the Reception facilities. Another alteration was the conversion of the Television Room – now virtually redundant thanks to the arrival of TV in the bedrooms – to an additional function room, initially called for want of a better name the Drawing Room. The name has stuck. The 1983 Newsletter subsequently reported that these many improvements had been accompanied by considerable expenditure on fire detection, containment and warning systems, emergency lighting and escape routes, and replacement of worn-out electrical and plumbing installations.

During these years of constant change and development the Committee never lost sight of the long-term implications of the eventual expiry of the Lease on the Club building. In 1971, during Basil Hamilton's time as Chairman, it had been agreed to have the Club valued with a view to negotiating purchase of the Lease from the owner, now Sutton Estates. The answer was £300,000 if the building remained a Club, £800,000 if it could be redeveloped, but it soon became clear that Sutton Estates were not prepared to sell the Freehold. Reluctant to give up too easily, Hamilton asked the President, Sir Dermot Boyle, to entertain Sir Robert and Lady Sutton to lunch in the hope of persuading him to intercede on the Club's behalf. 'Nothing of value resulted', reported Sir Dermot. The initiative then passed to the Central Fund, which in 1973 invited the Chairman to produce a paper seeking the Fund's assistance. As a result the Trustees agreed to establish a special reserve within the Fund designed to build up sufficient capital by 2019 for the purchase of permanent premises; to that end the Fund would contribute £20,000 per annum and the Club itself would place a further £5,000 per annum in a new Property Reserve Fund.

It was ten years later, in January 1984, that the Committee heard the momentous news that the freehold was being bought by Stockleigh PLC, and Flight Lieutenant John Briggs – his ear well to the ground as Vice-

Chairman – advised that the Club would be in a strong position to purchase it from the new owners. With the Lease still having 35 years to run, he said, and the annual ground rent meanwhile yielding only £3,000 per annum, the new owners might well prefer to cash in early. The Committee, led by Air Commodore Robert Wood, accordingly registered the Club's interest with Stockleigh, stating that no problems were envisaged in obtaining the necessary finance. Then in December word leaked out in the press about property deals on the north side of Piccadilly, and the *Daily Telegraph* referred to a crisis facing the Cavalry Club whose lease (which had much less time to run) might well not be renewed. Wood referred to this in the March Newsletter, assuring members that the RAF Club's position was in no way linked with that of the Cavalry Club. Meanwhile the Committee was brought up to date about the negotiations and agreed the financial arrangements. On 6 May the Directors of the RAF Club Company gave their approval and on the 23rd the AGM was informed that Stockleigh was willing to sell the Lease for £1.6 million, subject to the Charity Commission's approval. About half the money would be provided by the Central Fund. The rest would come from sale of the Club investments (bought from the former Lease Redemption Policy – see pp. 62 and 89) for £239,000, Club general funds, and a £400,000 bank loan repayable over four years. The AGM received the news with 'applause' and the contract was signed on 31 May. In the 1986 Newsletter Wood summarised the achievement.

> We owe much to the original generosity of Lord Cowdray who gave us the lease in 1921. We are no less indebted to the Trustees of the Central Fund who have for some years given us guidance and financial support. It represents an outstanding investment, but most significantly it secures our future as a Club.

So for the last 20 years the Club Committee and Management have been able to work in the knowledge that the possibility of dispossession no longer exists. They have been fortunate too in another way. In the 1980s in particular, faced with the necessity of repaying substantial loans in respect of the freehold and of major development schemes, they benefited from a national economic climate much more favourable than that of the 1970s. The signs were already promising in 1980, when the Newsletter reported for the first time total income exceeding a million pounds. A mere eight years later that sum had more than doubled. Throughout this period trading was buoyant, exemplified by bedroom occupancy rates usually well over 80 per cent, function business which generated up to 30 per cent of the Club's net income, and highly satisfactory catering and bar profits. True there were criticisms, notably from serving officers who thought the Club too expensive, but the Committee stood firm, pointing out that they could not hope to compete with Officers' Mess prices. They were aiming to maintain high standards in a particularly expensive part of London yet were still holding bar prices at 10 per cent below those of Mayfair pubs, and the Club's usage remained high. In any case substantial profits were essential if the necessary maintenance and improvements were to be continued.

The later 1980s witnessed further important projects. Work began in 1984 to install a fast lift midway between the front and rear bedroom areas; a much-needed improvement, this would for the first time allow wheelchair access to the bedroom floors. In 1986 extensive external maintenance was carried out, an external fire escape constructed, and more modern computer systems fitted in the front office and reception areas; and in 1987 plans were begun to add a number of new bedrooms on the fourth floor. The main work on these was carried out in 1989/90 while Air Commodore David Hawkins was Chairman, at a cost, including air conditioning and the new lift, of a million pounds. The 12 extra bedrooms, all doubles or twins, were formally opened by the President, Sir Lewis Hodges, in September 1990. The subsequent Newsletter described the marked effect of this expansion of the Club's facilities: the number of occasions when the Club was unable to offer accommodation had already been reduced by half. This was a fitting moment for James Swaffield to bow out as Secretary. He had officiated for 15 years, a period of great significance and success, and today's Club remains deeply indebted to him for all he did. He was offered and accepted Honorary Life Membership in January 1991.

The arrival of Swaffield's successor, Peter Owen, coincided with a somewhat changed situation, partly occasioned by the first Gulf War. When he took over, the Club's trading position had the healthy look that had applied throughout the 1980s, but in May 1991 the Committee had to take note of the serious impact of that war, together with the increasing activities of the IRA and a particularly severe winter. In July, while accommodation revenue remained excellent, Dining Room and Buttery income was declining. The February 1992 Newsletter reported bedroom usage down by 10 per cent, Dining Room, Running Horse and Buttery also lower, and only function income remaining buoyant. Clearly, not just in the Club but much more widely, there was a downturn in business and the trend seemed likely to continue. Fortunately, however, the Club was better placed than many other establishments to weather the storm.

One major step forward had been taken in 1988, under Richard Kyle's chairmanship, when the Committee decided to prepare a long-term financial plan to take effect once the bedroom extension had been paid for. Two of the initial recommendations of the small sub-committee then appointed were to establish a Property Renewal Fund and to obtain an accurate valuation of the building. The latter assessed the cost of replacement at £18 million, whereupon the insurance value was raised to £27 million. In this and other ways the Finance Sub-Committee was soon demonstrating its worth and enabling individual Committee members to contribute directly to financial planning. Since then several other sub-committees have also taken their places in the main committee structure, and the Secretary himself has been closely involved in their various activities. Financial control, in particular, has been much improved thanks to the computerisation of the accounts in 1993 and the much better presentation of information that became possible. The situation in the 1990s could so easily have been much worse than it was. As the 1995 Newsletter recorded, the marked reduction in the number of officers serving in the London area as a result of RAF cuts and reorganisation was bound to affect Club business, and the decline of bedroom occupancy to 62.5 per cent in 1994 was a serious blow, yet by 1997 occupancy was back to over 75 per cent, where it has remained ever since. Other sources of income – even functions – also caused anxiety early on, but the position has generally recovered. Good management, coupled with inventive ideas, has done much to compensate.

On the management front the new Secretary instituted fortnightly senior staff meetings in 1991 and the Committee agreed to introduce pay differentials for long-serving staff and for additional qualifications – though performance-related pay was ruled out. In 1993 a comprehensive staff training programme aimed at developing a professional team at all levels was begun, with Kathryn Cooper being placed in charge of personnel and training. At the same time control over immigrant staff was tightened after an employee had been arrested because of false papers. From then on all staff have been required to produce a birth certificate or other document to show they have the right to work. In 1995 the first three candidates began studying for National Vocational Qualifications (NVQs), followed by 11 more a year later. In 1997 the Club was accredited as an 'Investor in People', thus demonstrating the quality of its staff training and development programme, and an 'Employee of the Month' scheme was inaugurated. The Club's membership of the Club Secretaries and Managers' Association and of the Association of London Clubs has also yielded valuable training opportunities.

There was no let-up in the 1990s in the schemes for improving the Club's fabric and facilities. In 1991 the storage room at the rear of the main Dining Room was converted to a small private dining room, now called the Boardroom. In 1993 came the renovation of the Cowdray Room with a new bar, décor and furniture; at the same time full air-conditioning was installed in the Ballroom together with modern equipment for both conferences and banquets. It was time now to refurbish 33 of the older bedrooms, a task completed in 1994. The increasing demand for air conditioning in these and other areas had already been catered for by the fitting of new plant on the roof of the building; weighing some four tons, this was winched up on Saturday 15 August 1992 after Old Park Lane had been closed for the purpose.

In 1996 the hitherto somewhat ad hoc procedure for managing renovations and improvements was changed when a full-scale Finance Committee superseded the smaller sub-committee and introduced the concept of a Rolling Programme. This included in 1997 plans to refurbish fully the first-floor Drawing Room, to improve the ground-floor kitchen facilities and to make major changes in the basement area. In 1998 came the re-design of the main entrance area, refurbishment and air-conditioning of the Dining Room, and redecoration of the Reading Room, now to be redesignated the Library. The extensive basement work took longer to prepare for. The area in question had been profitably used since 1972 as the Buttery, but since the mid-1980s its trade had steadily declined and the Committee felt that the valuable space could be used more productively. So a scheme was drawn up to replace it with two state-of-the-art conference rooms and a study, which it was felt would be appreciated not least by members who wished to hold business meetings in the Club and thus bring in valuable trading income. So in January 2000, at an estimated cost of £1.7 million, the project was authorised. The facility had been completed by the end of the year and, as the Millennium Suite, has since proved highly successful. This provides an excellent example of the way the Club continues to expand its facilities as members' requirements change – indeed until the mid-1980s the Club had explicitly forbidden its use for business or professional purposes.

Another scheme, however, did not go ahead, despite having taken much Committee time. It arose in 1999 from high-level complaints that the Club could all too often still not meet members' requirements for bedroom accommodation. Several possible options were investigated and quickly rejected, including conversion of staff accommodation on the fifth floor, lease of a floor of the Cavalry and Guards Club, and acquisition of the freehold of the former Coutts Bank next door. Only the conversion of the Squash Courts into either 12 or 21 bedrooms was seen as realistic, but when the subject was debated at the 2000 AGM the Chairman promised to consult the squash players and the wider membership. The subsequent survey elicited replies from only five squash players and 25 other members, and it also became clear that the alleged shortage of rooms was based on anecdotal evidence rather than hard facts. So the scheme was deferred and remains so – just as it has been on earlier occasions in the Club's story. Meanwhile renovations have continued elsewhere, with several projects completed in 2002. The last 13 bedrooms on the fourth floor have been modernised, the Gentlemen's Cloakroom and basement lavatory area renovated, and the ground floor and first-floor corridors completely redecorated.

So in less than 40 years since the Colonels' Revolt, the Club has been virtually transformed, thanks not least to the active links that have been maintained at the highest levels with the RAF itself. Its finances are sound and its management is operated on far more professional lines. Carefully programmed refurbishment and maintenance are thoroughly carried out and of high quality, in sharp contrast with the ad hoc approach of the Club's first 45 years. Not surprisingly, therefore, these changes have had an immense impact upon its amenities and life.

CHAPTER 10

THE ACTIVE CLUB

The later 1960s and early 1970s witnessed relatively little change in the general pattern of the Club's activities. The 1966 Newsletter promoted it as a thriving centre and meeting place for the RAF in London, offering excellent facilities for the individual but also a variety of other functions – wedding receptions, cocktail parties, squadron reunions and so on. Specific Club gatherings, however, were – as in the past – few and far between, usually occasioned by special events. The first of these, a reception designed to celebrate the 50th Anniversary of the foundation of the RAF, took place in November 1968 in the presence of Her Majesty the Queen and the Duke of Edinburgh. The Royal visitors were most impressed by the Club building itself and by the recent growth in membership, as reflected in the 700 who attended and had had to be selected by ballot from a much larger number of applicants. This truly memorable event was seen as a fitting conclusion to the metamorphosis which had begun four years earlier.

Another great event was remembered in January 1972, when the 50th Anniversary of the opening of 128 Piccadilly was marked by a dinner attended among others by 60 members who had joined the Club before 1926, and four staff who had been with the Club in 1922. A few days later the Anniversary was again celebrated, but less formally, this time with an open invitation to 'drinks at 1922 prices'. A total of 116 bottles of whisky, 59 bottles of gin and 1,560 pints of beer were consumed. Another Royal visit followed in June, this time by the Queen Mother who herself had taken part in the original opening ceremony; then in October 1973 the Duchess of Gloucester attended the WRAF Officers' Association Annual Reunion.

No other major occasions are recorded during these years, and efforts to extend the general social facilities on offer to members were confined to the Discotheque. Its inception in 1968 owed much to the drive of Air Commodore Freddie Sowrey, who had strongly argued in the Hodges Committee the case for making the Club more attractive to the younger officers, and was now Chairman. At the 1965 EGM, in fact, Sowrey had memorably remarked that one idea for attracting young members was to provide them with some music and a pocket-handkerchief-sized floor where they could stand next to a girl and prop themselves up; this was called 'dancing'. Now, thanks not least to the enthusiastic support of one of his Committee members, Flight Lieutenant N. J. Galpin, the Ladies' Bar on the first floor was converted for the purpose and opened on 11 October 1968, with the barman and waitresses in Victorian dress. By early 1969 it was clear that younger officers were being attracted to the new venture, though there were already some anxieties about its control, particularly in relation to the licensing laws after 11 p.m.. A year later the Newsletter reported that the Victoria Disco was proving very popular and since it had outgrown the old bar on the first floor was to be moved to the basement. This would reduce the noise elsewhere in the Club, and the room would also serve as a daytime snack bar.

The basement disco was opened on 4 September 1970, with a doorkeeper employed to prevent non-members entering and a 4s. entrance charge being levied which would go towards the cost of a meal. Then in January 1971 came an unprecedented relaxation of the Club rules: jackets and ties could be removed, although they must be replaced before departure! In July, however, the Secretary felt obliged to express his anxieties about the way it was being run and from now on difficulties in finding a suitable manager and a good disc jockey contributed to its decline in popularity. By 1973 costs were no longer being covered and in October 1974 the Committee bit the bullet and closed the Disco.

Successful though the disco had been for a few years, it had really done little to help fulfil the charitable objects of the Club as agreed in 1967, and in 1971 a letter from the Chief Inspector of Taxes querying the Club's Charitable Status had already come as a warning shot. This asked what steps had been taken to carry out the assurances originally given, the general thrust being that the Club seemed to differ little from other London Clubs which were not charities. The Chairman had replied elaborating on the Club's value to the efficiency of the RAF and the Chief Inspector paid an informal visit in November. Finally in February 1972 he wrote that the Club would retain its Charitable Status and he could see no reason why it should be challenged in the foreseeable future.

This brush with the taxman had served to warn the Club against complacency about the financial value of Charitable Status, and when Robin Lees became Chairman in 1977 he immediately invited the Committee to consider ways of meeting the second of its four charitable objects, hitherto largely ignored:

> To encourage, by means of discussion, lectures, film shows, etc.,
> an interest in all matters connected with flying in general and with
> the RAF in particular.

This prompted Air Commodore Henry Probert, who had joined the Committee in 1974 and was now the RAF's Director of Educational Services, to offer to organise a lecture programme. Such was the demand for seats that the first event, a symposium on 'RAF Prospects for the next 20 years' conducted by the Director of Air Plans and the Director of Forward Policy, was held twice on different evenings in November 1977. Building on this success three more lectures were arranged in 1978; subjects included 'Modern Air Power' and 'The RAF in Germany' and each attracted 200 or more members. Publicised in the Newsletter and elsewhere, the programme continued well into the 1980s, though with widely varying responses, and mainly attracting retired members who wanted to keep in touch with current Service matters. Thanks to Probert's growing connections with RAF history (he had become Head of the Air Historical Branch (RAF) at the end of 1978), a number of historical subjects were included in the programme, and in 1981 came the first of several well-attended film shows. The last really popular lecture took place in 1985, when Air Marshal Sir John Curtiss and Group Captain Peter Squire spoke about the Falklands Conflict to an audience of 120. In October 1987, however, an excellent talk by Air Commodore Ted Williams on 'The Soviet Union Today' attracted a mere 40 and the Committee reluctantly decided it was time to draw the line. It had in mind not just poor attendances, but also the recent formation of the RAF Historical Society which a number of Club members had already joined. Close ties have since been maintained with the Society, which holds its committee meetings and some of its lectures in the Club.

Running in parallel with the Club lecture programme were Club Dinners, originating from John Briggs' suggestion in October 1977 to hold regular Guest Nights with visiting speakers. This led to a proposal to form a Dining Society; publicised in the March 1978 Newsletter, it generated widespread support and the inaugural dinner was held the following November in celebration of the Club's 60th Anniversary. In the chair was John Briggs and the Guest Speaker was Sir Michael Beetham, Chief of Air Staff. To mark the occasion, a Message of Loyal Greeting had been sent to the Queen, eliciting a warm reply. A second dinner was promptly arranged in March 1979, with the Lord Mayor of Westminster as speaker, and as the Dining Society's membership was now nearing 500 a pattern of four dinners per year was adopted; in November 1981 the attendance reached 140, the maximum capacity of the Ballroom. At this stage some Club members were saying that the atmosphere of the dinners was being spoilt by allowing wives to attend, but the Dining Society Committee decided against making any change. Ever since then the Society evenings have remained firmly established in the annual calendar, with attendances averaging over 100. The Presidency has changed every few years: Tony Iveson took over from Briggs in 1980, succeeded in turn by Leonard Williams (then Club Vice-Chairman), Bill Beaumont, Geoff Claridge and Matt Wiles, and other Committee members have assisted the Club staff with many of the arrangements. Altogether more than a hundred well-known guest speakers have so far addressed the Society, usually responding to questions afterwards; they have been drawn from many walks of life, including aviation, industry, the professions, national and international politics, and of course the RAF and other Armed Services. As Club Chairman, Henry Hall, wrote in the 1994 Newsletter, the Dining Society's activities were perhaps in the forefront of fulfilling the objectives of the Club.

The Chairman was in fact referring to more than just the evening dinners. In September 1991 the Committee had agreed that the Dining Society should also hold lunch-time events in the hope of attracting members who worked in London but were unable or unwilling to come along in the evenings. So on 22 June 1992 Wing Commander J. A. Broadbent, who had commanded the Tornado Squadron in the recent Gulf War, spoke at the first such lunch; so successful was this that similar occasions, often addressed by COs of operational units, have been held two or three times a year ever since. In a sense these maintain the tradition established by the evening lectures of the 1980s.

The 1990s also witnessed the inclusion in the Club's programme of various speciality dinners, organised by the newly formed Events Committee, initially led by Tony Banks and later by Keith Garratt. The first of what have become regular Gourmet Dinners took place in 1995, with 43 members attacking a six- or seven-course menu washed down with selected wines and all introduced by either the Chef or the wine merchant. In 1997 came an even more expensive 'Menu Gastronomique'. Costing £80 per head and with attendance limited to 18 members so as to allow more discussion of the food and wines, this periodic event was subsequently re-titled the 'Fine Wine Dinner'. The first of various theme dinners was held in 1999, in the form of a Curry Evening for which Pat Chapman, the founder of the UK Curry Club and himself a full Club member, was placed in charge of the kitchens for the night. 'From flying to frying, from pilot to popadom' joked the Newsletter afterwards. The Oriental flavour continued in 2000, this time devoted to Thai cuisine.

There were also larger functions marking particular anniversaries, for example VE Day and VJ Day lunches in 1995; both offered menus at 7s. 6d., with food reflecting what had been available at the time, and were sold out. In 1997 a Battle of Britain Reception was introduced, soon followed by a Members' Christmas Lunch, both subsequently becoming regular parts of the social calendar. So over-subscribed was the latter that since 1998 two lunches have been held on successive days, each attended by some 200 members. Carol-singing by the choir of St Clement Danes has contributed to the festive atmosphere. December 2003 witnessed another innovation when the Club hosted a pantomime for members' children accompanied by refreshments and a visit to Father Christmas. The event was over-subscribed and may well find a permanent place in the Club's social calendar. On a smaller scale regular early-evening receptions enabling Committee members to welcome new Club members have been held since 1996 and are much appreciated.

In the 1990s the Committee also decided that it was time to revive one of the Club's older traditions. New Year's Eve dances had been held both before the war and in the 1950s, with varying success, and an abortive attempt to restart them had been made in 1973. Not until 1991 was the subject raised again when, at the AGM, a member urged a function open to everyone in order to reinforce the Club atmosphere. The Chairman, Air Commodore David Davies, subsequently called for views and asked for volunteers to organise and promote the concept. So on 22 October 1992, the 70th Anniversary of the opening of the Club building, 248 members and their guests attended a highly successful Club Ball. The Newsletter paid special tribute to the workers: the transformation of so many rooms into elegant dining areas and a ballroom, and their restoration for breakfast the next morning was an excellent achievement by the staff.* The event was repeated in June 1993, with 215 attending; considered a

---

* The 60th Anniversary in 1982 had been recognised with a Club Reception, which was well reported by Peterborough in the *Daily Telegraph*.

'magnificent evening', it led to the decision to hold further Balls each autumn. Yet by 1995 support was clearly waning, leading to a £1,300 deficit, and the Chairman, Air Commodore Henry Hall, commented that the event appeared expensive to serving officers and its format had become routine. Nevertheless, the annual Balls continued, albeit on a smaller scale, until 1999, when against a target of 150 only 117 members and guests attended. In 2000 the Ball – now seen as unlike present-day Officers' Mess Balls – was re-styled as a Dinner Dance yet attracted only 108. The Committee then decided that future marketing should include an approach to members who might wish to use the occasion for corporate entertainment. Colonel Bersey and his contemporaries would have turned in their graves! In fact the Club Ball was to be resuscitated in 2002 (see below), albeit as a 'one-off'.

The real successes in recent years have been the major anniversary celebrations, though the elaborate plans set in hand to mark the RAF's 75th Anniversary in 1993 did not entirely come up to expectations. Hopes that Her Majesty the Queen would be able to attend were dashed, and the intending writing and publication of a Club history was impossible in the time scale. The event that did materialise was a major dinner for 193 members on 25 September, preceded by a reception attended by 137 more. Four years later, however, the Chairman, Air Vice-Marshal Peter Dodworth, was able to announce that the 75th Anniversary of the official opening of the Club building by the Duke of York was to be marked by a Reception hosted by the President, Sir Michael Beetham. 'We are honoured', Dodworth wrote, 'that Her Majesty Queen Elizabeth the Queen Mother has graciously consented to be present.' This was a truly memorable occasion, at which the Guest of Honour, now well into her nineties and seemingly tireless, spoke so graciously to far more people than one would have thought possible.

Then in 2002 came an even larger-scale event – or series of events – for the 80th Anniversary. At the instance of the Chairman, Air Vice-Marshal Phil Roser, five functions were held, starting with the second of what have now become annual Club Church Services at St Clement Danes. This took place on Sunday 24 February in the presence of the Duke of York, and was followed by an Anniversary Lunch. Two days later there was a Gala Reception, enjoyed by 183 members. On the 27th the President and Committee hosted a formal dinner, at which Mess Dress was worn, to acknowledge the support given to the Club by the RAF and its associated organisations; attendance was by invitation only and the 95 who were there included officers of all ranks from a wide range of RAF units. The Chief of Air Staff responded to the toast to the RAF. On 1 March came a Gala Ball, with 179 present, and last but by no means least a Reception was held on 5 March for the staff on whose unstinted efforts the success of the whole week's activities had depended.

The new century has already been marked in other ways too. Back in 1972 the Committee had considered organising theatre parties at special rates including a meal in the Club, and the idea had been dropped after enquiries had indicated lack of interest, but 30 years later the idea has been re-floated and is proving popular. Organised visits to places of interest in or near London have also taken off after a highly successful sortie to nearby Apsley House in 2000, and in 2003 an initial trip to the First World War battlefields on the continent was also well supported.

Within the Club itself a new amenity has arrived in the shape of a Library. While there is mention of a Club library in the pre-war records, it does not appear to have become a major feature and was more often described as the Writing – or Reading – Room. In 1932, such books as the Club possessed were not all even in that Room. After the war the newspapers, magazines and a few general reference books in the Reading Room were the nearest approach to a proper library. In 2001, however, after Mrs Jinny Wootton offered to donate her late husband's 225 RAF and general aviation books to the Club (see Chapter 11), volunteer members were recruited to help sort, catalogue and monitor the collection, and donations were solicited from other members. By 2003 new shelving had been fitted in the Reading Room (funded out of a £42,000 legacy from Margaret Elizabeth Pugh, the widow of a former member), many more books had been donated, and a team of five members had worked assiduously with support from Club staff to arrange the 900 books now on charge into a proper reference library with scope for expansion and further development. It was formally opened by Jinny Wootton on 25 September in the presence of Air Chief Marshal Sir Jock Stirrup, Chief of Air Staff. Strangely, at that very moment the fate of the original library books was revealed. They were at the RAF Museum, to whose new library they had been loaned at the suggestion of Freddie Sowrey, when the Museum was being prepared for its opening in 1972. Sir Dermot Boyle may also have had a hand in this, for not only was he Club President but also first Chairman of the

Museum's Trustees! Most of the books, including several relating to the Cowdray family, are now being returned to the Club.

The last 30 years of the Club's story have also seen the resuscitation of the two traditional sporting activities, golf and squash. It was Group Captain B. A. J. Crummy who in 1971 was given permission to restart the Golf Society and organised the inaugural match at West Hill on 19 October. Its success prompted the Club to enter a team once again in the Bath Golf Club Cup (see Chapter 3), since when the Society has continued its annual matches, which these days attract 30–40 members. From 1980 onwards teams have also been entered for the Bath Cup and won it several times. Ever since 1973 the Society's fortunes have been described in the Newsletter which in 1986 paid due tribute to Crummy's organising abilities over the previous 15 years.

The Squash players too have long had their Bath Club competition, and when in 1975 the Club team was promoted to the First Division the Committee – aware that its own courts were not competition size – agreed to pay the expenses of court hire when the team had to play home matches on its opponents' courts. The subsequent story has been one of mixed fortunes. On average some 20 members have been regular players including at times some of top-class, but thanks to the vagaries of RAF postings and the long distances some have needed to travel it has always been hard to keep together teams able to compete at high level. Nor has the Club been able to afford to do as much as the players would have liked in order to modernise the courts. Nevertheless, in 2002 the Newsletter could describe the Bath Club team as enjoying its most successful season for many years, having won 9 of 16 matches and looking to finish in the top half of Division Two – something not achieved for at least 10 years.

More recent years have also seen the Club trying to become more 'user-friendly'. The rules governing the admission of children were one concern as evidenced in the 1968 Newsletter. This recognised the desire of members visiting London to bring their families and announced the reduction of the minimum age limit from fourteen to ten for a trial period. A year later the limit was lowered to eight. In 1975, however, a more radical proposal to admit children of all ages was firmly rejected as likely to lose the Club more members than it gained. Then six years later the limit was reduced to five with the proviso that on arrival members would be given a statement of the guidelines for the control and conduct of their children. The rules have since been liberally interpreted to the extent that the 1997 Newsletter said that 'contrary to common belief children and babies under five are welcome to stay in the Club at weekends and public holidays'. The Club's transformation into a family-friendly and extremely attractive venue from which to explore London has helped to increase the number of Clubs with which it has entered into reciprocal arrangements, both at home and overseas. The list is regularly reviewed and there are now 37 of them. Not only are these facilities attractive to present-day young officers, but they also further the charitable objects of the Club in providing opportunities to meet and associate with officers of other Air Forces and other Services. Nor should the Club's links with another charity be forgotten: the RAF Benevolent Fund. The Fund's diffi-culties in meeting the ever-increasing demands on its resources prompted a donation of £5,000 in 1987, and two years later a major appeal from the Controller led to individual members contributing some £76,000. The Club itself has made annual donations ever since.

Another vexed issue has been that of dress. In the 1970s, as many serving members pointed out, officers' messes were becoming much more relaxed about the wearing of suits and sports jackets, and the Club had to strike an increasingly delicate balance. On the one hand the younger officers wanted greater informality; on the other, many of the older members – who brought the Club so much of its business – wished to preserve similar standards to those of most other London clubs. The Committee itself was at times deeply divided on this matter and not until 1978 did the opening of the Running Horse prompt a decision to widen the interpretation of the rule 'properly dressed at all times' to mean 'a jacket at all times with a tie or cravat or a roll-neck shirt of single colour in thin smooth material'. In 1982, considering a committee member's complaint on behalf of other members about over-stringent dress standards, the Committee agreed that the 1978 revision had gone far enough; a year later it remained unmoved in relation to the request for shirt-sleeve order during very hot weather. The 1984 AGM even suggested that the rules were not being firmly enough applied; jackets, for example, were being interpreted as cardigans and bomber-jackets and – heaven forbid – some ladies were getting away with T-shirts, jeans and sneakers. Not until 1992 did a new message really start to get across, when relaxed dress was allowed in the Running Horse at weekends and in the Dining Room for breakfast, and in 1995 the weekend relaxation was extended to the Cowdray Room.

In 1991 another welcome change appeared. For several years pressure had been building up for the Club to accept payment by debit and credit cards, but the administrative and commission costs to the Club had been thought to outweigh the benefits. In 1990, however, debit cards were agreed to and the Vice-Presidents collectively recommended that credit cards should follow. So in May 1991 the Committee agreed to go ahead provided that satisfactory commission could be negotiated and in August Visa and Mastercard arrived on the scene, much to most members' satisfaction.

Merchandising of Club products has been greatly extended in recent years. While it began with the sale of Christmas Cards in 1930, its growth as a significant part of the Club's business operation dates from the introduction of a Club tie in 1978. This idea had first been floated in 1927 and more recently in 1956, when it was quickly pooh-poohed (p. 74). The first serious proposal, from Wing Commander Manwaring in 1967, resulted in a notice being placed in the Gentlemen's Bar asking for suggested designs. Only one response appeared and in 1969 the idea was dropped, together with ideas for a Club Diary and a Club Wallet. In 1973 the Committee felt that since Club ties were no longer fashionable the RAF Club need not have one, and in 1974 station representatives reported little interest among the RAF at large. In January 1978, however, the Committee took a more positive line and enquiries led in September to an order for a thousand red, dark blue and light blue striped silk ties for sale at £3 each. Each Committee member received a complimentary one and was asked to wear it on all possible occasions. Soon afterwards a cheaper Terylene version was also ordered and, prompted by the Newsletter, sales took off. Since then additional designs have been introduced and following on the arrival of a Club Diary many more Club products have been developed, for ladies as well as gentlemen. Advertised through the Newsletters and on sale by mail (including email) and in the recently established Club Shop, some 40 items are now available.

Amid the success story of more recent years, the Committee has never lost sight of the growing possibility of terrorist attack. The first scare occurred in June 1972, when a hoax phone call at 11 p.m. stated that a bomb was set to explode at midnight and the duty manager evacuated all residents for the next hour. Three years later, aware of mounting threat assessments in Central London, the Committee introduced various security measures, including fitting anti-shatter film on the Piccadilly windows, removing window boxes, restricting the front entry route and checking membership cards, and placing security staff on duty at busy times. In the 1975 Newsletter members were asked to bear with restrictions such as baggage checks and to accept the Committee's regrets should the entrance hall at times resemble the Left Luggage Office at Waterloo Station. That the dangers were real was evident in the 1976 comment that bombs at the Hilton and the Green Park Underground had been too close for comfort. Subsequently threat levels have varied, but were perhaps highest in 1990 at the time of the bombing of the Carlton Club, when a further bomb hoax led to the Club's closure to allow a thorough police search. As a result the Committee accepted a proposal by the Royal British Legion Attendants Company to provide full-time security cover, but given the high cost and the limitations of the service being provided this arrangement did not last long. Then in 1993, following terrorist attacks in the City of London, supplementary insurance cover to protect the premises had to be taken out and this effectively doubled the premium. Fortunately such costs have since fallen, but the threat remains and the Club maintains close links with the police, particularly through 'Club Watch', a group of Club Managers who meet them at least once a quarter.

Security of the Club's property and that of members is another abiding concern. In 1968, thefts from bedrooms and lockers led to the Committee seeking advice from Securicor and the RAF Police. They had scarcely had time to report than the Cellar was broken into and cash went missing from the Reception safe. As a result a security officer was appointed (jointly with the Carlton Club), with responsibility for physical security of the building, safeguarding of members' property, carrying out spot checks, and advising the Secretary on security matters. Soon afterwards an intruder was caught in the act of stealing a coat from the Gentlemen's Cloakroom, and in 1970 it was agreed to install a Paralock coat rack system. This proved generally successful, though on one occasion in 1973 the system failed to defeat an attack by an intruder wielding a crowbar. Other types of theft also worried members in the 1970s, causing complaints at the ease with which non-members could gain access to the Club rooms. The Committee's answer was to promise periodic spot checks on everyone entering the building and to urge all members to carry their Club cards. There has always been a balance to be struck between close control and the desirability of a relaxed Club atmosphere, and the precautions taken have normally taken account of the nature of particular events and, of course, cost. One major innovation came in 1989 when following on the theft of a Chippendale Mirror valued at £650, a video monitoring system was installed to cover the front door, the reception area and the rear entrance. This has since been updated to include the concept of digital recording.

There have, too, been attempts at fraud. In 1975, for example, a Canadian claiming to be a member of the Royal Canadian Military Institution was issued with an Honorary Member's card and used it to obtain credit and cash cheques; the Club was instrumental in having him arrested. In 1992 an attempt was made to defraud the Club of £150,000 by an international telegraph transfer to Spain bearing the forged signatures of the Secretary and the Accountant; the alert Bank Manager spotted it in time. Members as well have caused problems. In 1981 a flight lieutenant who had misbehaved and caused disturbances on several occasions, not least when seeking entry to the Club during the night and insulting the night porter, was required to resign. The same thing happened in 1990 to an officer from overseas who also verbally abused the staff, attempted to break into the Club and damaged the front door, and refused to pay his bill. Perhaps even worse were a member and his wife who stayed in the Club seven weeks in 1988 and left without settling their £3,200 account; the Committee – belatedly – now set a credit limit of £500 for all bedroom accounts.

To round off this particular theme a unique incident which occurred in 1973 is worth recounting. On 24 October a long-standing member, Group Captain Dudley Saward, brought into the Club for lunch Hitler's former Armaments Minister, Albert Speer. They had got to know each other in Germany when Saward was doing research for his forthcoming biography of Sir Arthur 'Bomber' Harris, and Speer – released from Spandau Prison in 1966 – had agreed to discuss the effects of the RAF bombing campaign. Speer had then come to London to take part in a television programme and Saward had offered to show him round the city. Inevitably, however, the press were on to the story as soon as he landed at Heathrow, where he was held by immigration officials for eight hours before the Home Secretary gave permission for a two-day stay. So when Speer and Saward reached the Club the Daily Express reporters among others were not far behind. Next day, reporting the visit, the paper referred to Saward's work on Harris's biography and quoted Edward Jeffreys' statement, as Secretary, that the Club had not been told that Speer would be a guest. 'If members were unsure about whether guests would be acceptable they contacted the Committee beforehand,' Jeffreys had said.

Five days later the Executive Committee was put in the picture and told that 16 members had protested about the visit, some offering to resign. It agreed that Saward should be required to explain himself before a small sub-committee. The General Committee was more bullish. 'If Saward had organised or assisted with the publicity over the visit which might be of value to his book, a serious view should be taken.' Saward responded in writing: he was not willing to give his reasons for inviting Speer and preferred to resign his membership, which the Committee accepted. Its reasons were the suspicion that Saward had intended the visit and its associated publicity to promote his book, and also Speer's unsuitability as a visitor in the light of the Nuremberg Trials. No such difficulties attended the stay in the Club later that month of Luftwaffe General Galland, who was by then on the best of terms with his erstwhile RAF opponents.

There were two postscripts to this story. In November 1979 Saward (whose book was still unpublished) wrote to enquire if he could visit the Club as a member's guest and if he could be re-elected as a member; the Committee responded favourably and said there would be no entrance fee. Then in March 1981 Speer wrote to Harris – now an Honorary Member of the Club – who had expressed disappointment that Speer would not be coming to England so that they could meet: 'I vividly recall the experience during my last visit there that I had with the press and mass media, following me everywhere I went, including when Mr Saward took me to the Royal Air Force Club for lunch. I am sure you appreciate that I am anxious to avoid a repeat performance.'*

---

* This letter is in Harris's papers at the RAF Museum.

CHAPTER 11

TODAY'S IMAGE

More than eighty years ago the Club moved into 128 Piccadilly. Today's members may well reflect on the ways in which a balance has since been struck between some of its original features and the many improvements which have been so essential to its survival – and to its continuing success. In some ways, however, it is on first-time visitors that it creates the most vivid impression. In the basement they will find the Running Horse, with its traditional pub-style atmosphere, contrasting strongly with the ultra-modern conference and study facilities in the Millennium Suite. On the ground floor are the Club Bar, essentially providing for the more thirsty members, the newly developing Library to which the Bar gives access, and the Dining Room, which caters for all tastes in relatively formal and prestigious surroundings. Above is the comfortable and capacious Cowdray Room and Bar which offers light refreshments in a relaxed environment and commands a striking view across Piccadilly to Green Park. Then there are the various function rooms ranging from the small and welcoming Mezzanine Suite to the Drawing Room, the Presidents' Room and its accompanying Victoria Bar, and the spectacular Ballroom with capacity for major dinners and events of many other kinds. Few who enter the Club fail to admire the décor and the style with which it is all presented, and those who stay overnight also appreciate the quality of the bedroom accommodation, all well up to modern standards and making the best use of the inevitably restricted space available on the upper floors.

Of prime importance too are the staff, whose professional abilities, attitudes and enthusiasm set the tone. Some have been with the Club for many years and – taking their lead from such figures as the Head Porter – do their best to provide the kind of welcome that members so much appreciate. Many others are inevitably fairly short-term and bring to the Club an international flavour akin to that of most other London Clubs and similar establishments. All are encouraged to acquire some knowledge and understanding of the traditions and practices of the RAF – most important given the nature of so many of the functions that take place in the Club and the backgrounds of most of the members. It is they who set the tone when members and visitors arrive and start to take advantage of the many facilities.

Accompanying the friendly welcome are immediate indications of the RAF traditions enshrined in the Club, and it would be difficult on entering not to spot the Jubilee Gates that stand immediately ahead. In earlier years it was simple to walk straight through into the Long Corridor, but in 1976 it was decided in the interests of security to make entry easier to control by obstructing the route with a pair of ornamental wrought-iron gates; as a bonus these would be designed as a memorial of the Queen's Silver Jubilee. Initial drawings were obtained from Kentish Ironcraft at an estimated cost of £1,450. One of the Vice-Presidents, Air Chief Marshal Sir Ruthven Wade, then suggested that they be manufactured at RAF St Athan, and the Committee decided that the slightly higher cost would be justified by the prestige of having the work done 'in-house'. Installation was completed in September 1977 with the total bill of £1,698 being fully covered by members' subscriptions. The Gates were ceremonially opened by the President on 1 November and afterwards the Queen replied to his Loyal Greetings by expressing her appreciation, as the Club Patron, of the way in which her Silver Jubilee had been commemorated.

Hardly is the visitor past the Gates than he becomes aware of part of the Club's extensive art collection, which has been steadily built up over the years and constitutes a remarkable reflection of the history and traditions of the Royal Air Force to which the Club owes so much. Pictures and other artefacts are displayed throughout the building, the whole enterprise being directed by the Fine Arts Sub-Committee originally formed in 1978. Hitherto, pursuing the broad policy decided upon in the early 1950s (p. 66), the Committee had continued to acquire aircraft paintings usually through donations; in 1968, for example, a Sunderland came from Short and Harlands, a Lancaster from Hawker-Siddeley, a Spitfire from the British Aircraft Corporation, and a Boulton Paul Overstrand from 101 Squadron. Encouraged by such generosity, the Committee then investigated the possibility of buying one new painting each year and the coincident foundation of the Guild of Aviation Artists in 1971 offered the Club an invaluable entrée into this esoteric world. The Guild's Exhibition, held in London every July, has been attended ever since by Committee Members who have viewed the paintings, met many of the artists and on occasion bought paintings or commissioned new ones. Thirty years on, in 2002, the Club's association with the Guild has been further strengthened by its becoming a Friend.

The Fine Arts Sub-Committee was first chaired by Colin Kunkler and, in more recent years, Brian Moxey, John Burningham and the Vice-Chairman, Geoff Claridge, have played leading roles. They have given much thought on how best to develop the collection, trying to ensure that it is as comprehensive and representative as possible, and that it covers not just the RAF's early years and the ever popular Second World War topics but also later events as they have unfolded, together with more modern aircraft. They have regularly advised on where to hang the paintings, together with prints and photographs, using suitable wall space throughout the Club ranging from the basement areas to the upper bedroom floors. They have pursued a variety of ways to acquire further items, sometimes borrowing them, sometimes accepting donations, sometimes by paying for them either through Club funds or appealing to members and other benefactors for contributions towards specific projects. On occasion they have also sold items which have been considered surplus and devoted the proceeds to buying others of greater significance.

In selecting new paintings the Sub-Committee has firmly reverted to the 1920 policy of avoiding personalities, with the sole exception of its own Presidents. This practice had originated in 1922 with the painting of Lord Cowdray. While the 2nd and 3rd Lords Cowdray were not accorded the same privilege, by the time Sir John Salmond became President in 1945 his portrait – painted by Cuthbert Orde in 1932 – was already on display. So on his death in 1968 it was a natural step to feature his successor, Sir Dermot Boyle. His portrait, commissioned by the Club, was painted by Carlos Sancha and unveiled at a cocktail reception on 24 March 1971. Seven years later the Fine Arts Committee, deciding to face the question of where such pictures should be hung, recommended that the Drawing Room on the First Floor should be re-named the Presidents' Room for this purpose. Lord Cameron's portrait by Norman Hepple was the first to be unveiled there, on 17 December 1981, and the associated reception also marked the 60th Anniversary of the opening of the building. On 28 March 1987, Sir Lewis Hodges' portrait by Leonard Boden joined the group; its unveiling by Lady Boyle prompted the Newsletter comment that here 'in pride of place in the Presidents' Room were the portraits of the three members who rescued and revitalised the Club when our fortunes were waning in the 1960s'. With the arrival of another presidential portrait, that of Sir Michael Beetham, painted by

John Walton in 1994, there was no longer space for them all in the same room, so Hodges was moved to the Cowdray Room to join Her Majesty the Queen and Lord Cowdray. Then in 2002 Lord Craig's portrait painted by Richard Smyly replaced that of Beetham, who in turn has also found his place in the Cowdray Room.

Notwithstanding the general policy, most of the portraits which the Club obtained in earlier years remain on display. The Dining Room plays host to Lord Trenchard and Sir Winston Churchill. The Drawing Room features one of the RAF's wartime Chaplains-in-Chief, the Right Reverend J. A. Jagoe, together with several officers of the inter-war years, including Sefton Brancker. King Hussein of Jordan is there too; his portrait was badly damaged by an intruder in 1975 – maybe for political reasons – and while being repaired was found to have been a photograph with a painting superimposed. A second and particularly fine portrait of Sir Sefton Brancker, painted by Sir John Lavery in 1922, hangs in the Mezzanine Suite.

The Club's associations with the Royal Family, primarily represented by the Queen's portrait in the Cowdray Room, are also reflected elsewhere in the Club. In the Mezzanine is Norman Hoad's painting of the Queen's Colour Presentation to the Royal Auxiliary Air Force at Benson on 12 June 1989, and just outside are two well-known photographs of the RAF Review at Mildenhall by King George V on 6 July 1935. A painting of the Queen's Silver Jubilee Review of 29 July 1977 at Finningley is in the Victoria Bar Lobby, accompanied by photographs featuring the Duke of Edinburgh, Queen Elizabeth the Queen Mother, Prince Charles and Princess Anne.

The main art collection centres on several particularly significant paintings displayed in the central area of the Club. One of these, located at the foot of the front stairway, is Michael Turner's depiction of RAF Gatow at the time of the Berlin Airlift. This was commissioned in 1980 partly to remind members and visitors that other paintings showing the RAF fighting the Luftwaffe did not reflect the whole story of Anglo-German relations; it was based on photographs and records made available by the Air Historical Branch. The painting was unveiled on 1 April 1982 by Dr Richard von Weizsacker, the Governing Mayor of West Berlin (and later President of West Germany), and in the presence of a substantial number of RAF veterans of the Airlift. By remarkable coincidence the ceremony took place just as the news was breaking that

Argentine forces had landed in the Falklands, and among the veterans was Air Marshal Sir John Curtiss, who would soon be appointed Air Commander for the campaign to recover the islands.

Soon afterwards an even more ambitious project was embarked upon. It centred on the distinguished aviation artist Frank Wootton, who had been elected an Honorary Member of the Club in 1974 and had subsequently lent several of his finest paintings. In 1983, Colin Kunkler, who had been considering how better to use the Club's prime display area, the landing at the top of the main staircase, floated the idea that Wootton be commissioned to paint three great wartime scenes. One would show air combat over the trenches in the First World War, the second the Battle of Britain, the third air support on D-Day. The first theme was subsequently revised in discussion with Wootton so as to feature SE5a fighters of 56 Squadron on a French airfield and the second was readily accepted. The third, however, was switched, at the urging of Henry Probert, to portray what would almost certainly remain for ever the longest, most costly and most controversial campaign ever waged by the RAF: the bomber offensive against Germany.

For this the challenge would be to select an operation typical of those carried out by the Main Force of Bomber Command and which would – unlike most of them – be generally regarded as uncontroversial. Here the attack on Peenemünde, the V-weapon research establishment, on 17/18 August 1943, seemed to fill the bill, and fortuitously Air Commodore John Searby, who had led the raid as Master Bomber – and was a former Club Chairman (p. 73) – was still around and might be willing to be consulted. The Committee agreed to go ahead, Searby provided his audiotaped account of the attack and then visited Wootton while his work was in progress and advised on the technical detail. The result was a painting which is as authentic as it could possibly be and has with permission been widely reproduced abroad as well as at home. Sadly Searby died soon afterwards, but the painting survives in the Club as a permanent memorial to him and to the multitude of his comrades who flew during the war in Bomber Command, 55,000 of whom gave their lives.

All three of these great Wootton paintings were initially hung on the first floor as planned, though today only two remain there; the third, featuring the SE5s, now occupies the most prominent position in the Club Bar. In the corridor outside resides another particularly important

Wootton, the Triptych which was unveiled by Air Chief Marshal Sir Christopher Foxley-Norris at the first Battle of Britain Reception on 19 September 1997; in 1999 this exhibit, hitherto on loan, was donated to the Club on behalf of the Moffat Trust, which had bought it with money left in the will of a former wartime flying instructor. At about the same time, the Club was facing up to the implications of Frank Wootton's death in 1998. While some of his paintings on display belonged to the Club, others had been on loan and now had to be returned to Jinny, his widow. So after lengthy discussion the Committee decided to launch a major Art Appeal aiming to raise £50,000 for a Fund to procure specialist aviation fine art. Then in July 1998 Geoff Claridge visited Jinny to discuss her family's future relations with the Club and the Fine Art Appeal; she, convinced that the Club was the best location for her late husband's paintings, now generously agreed to return them. Subsequently, in 2000 – by which time the Arts Appeal, including legacies and gifts, was approaching £200,000 – she agreed to be co-opted to the Fine Arts Committee, and in 2001 offered to donate to the Club her husband's collection of aviation books (see p. 120). Altogether the Club now displays more than 30 of Frank Wootton's paintings, two-thirds of them portraying aircraft and associated themes from the Second World War and one – the SE5s – the First World War. The remainder feature post-war operations, including 'Vulcan Scramble' (a vivid reminder of the 1960s when Bomber Command constituted the nation's deterrent force), 'Sea Harrier over the Falklands' and 'Gulf War Tornados'.

While no other artist has contributed on anything like this scale, the Club is deeply indebted to numerous distinguished painters whose aircraft pictures are also displayed. Alan Fearnley stands out particularly by virtue of the three historic scenes he depicts in the Ballroom: DH9As patrolling over Arabia in the 1920s, the Southampton flying-boats arriving at Singapore in 1928, and Phantoms patrolling over the North Sea oil rigs in the 1970s. To these must be added the wartime Sunderland setting course to the West, and the portrayal of a Lancaster bringing food to the starving people of the Netherlands in Operation 'Manna'. This was unveiled in 1995 to mark the 50th Anniversary of that great errand of mercy.

Other distinguished artists represented include David Shepherd with his Harrier and his '21 Squadron Scramble' (also notable as his first wildlife painting), and Ray Nockolds with his evocative paintings of a

Sunderland, a Lancaster and a Spitfire dogfight, which are displayed in the Club Bar. Near them is a particularly unusual picture from the First World War, featuring a young boy whose portrait was rescued by members of the RFC Fifth Brigade from a village on the River Somme and used by them as a mascot – suitably embellished with officer's cap and RFC wings. In the corridor just outside hangs L. R. Urwin's pair of watercolours commemorating those who gave their lives in the air in the Battle of Britain, and downstairs, outside the Running Horse, is another memorial exhibit of a very different kind. Donated in 2003, this limited edition print features the 1943 events at Stalag Luft III which led to the Great Escape and the murder of 50 of the prisoners who had been recaptured. At the top of the stairs, in marked contrast, is another evocative scene. Painted by Keith Woodcock with advice from the crew involved, this portrays Black Buck 1, the 1982 Vulcan operation to bomb the Port Stanley runway, made possible by in-flight refuelling over the South Atlantic.*

A different artistic medium, sculpture, has also featured in recent years, to an extent substituting for personal portraits. The first post-war bust to arrive on the scene was that of Sir Barnes Wallis, to whose many design skills the RAF owed so much, particularly in the Second World War. Sculpted by Marcus Kaye, it was donated by Wallis himself in 1975 and received at an informal lunch. A second most distinguished engineer was similarly honoured in 1994, after the Fine Arts Sub-Committee had decided to purchase James Butler's bust of Sir Frank Whittle, the inventor of the jet engine. His son, Ian, after visiting the Club, had secured the backing of Rolls-Royce and Esso in meeting the cost. At the unveiling, Air Commodore Henry Hall, the Club Chairman, mentioned that it was on the Club's notepaper that Sir Rolf Dudley-Williams had written in 1935 the letter that duly led to the industrial development of the jet engine in England. Butler's work was featured again in 2002, when the Appeal Fund financed a bust of R. J. Mitchell, the designer of the Spitfire, which was unveiled at the 80th Anniversary Reception (p. 119). Also received by the Club from the Southampton Hall of Aviation was a framed record of the first Spitfire flight, carried out by Mutt Summers, and among the distinguished gathering was one of the first test pilots, Alex Henshaw. A year later came similar recognition for the designer of the Lancaster, Roy

---

* The locations of paintings, etc., mentioned in this chapter are correct at the time of going to press.

Chadwick, whose bust by Butler was paid for by the remainder of the Pugh legacy (p. 120) and equally warmly received. All four busts are displayed in the Club's ground floor corridor and suitably safeguarded; the Club wants no repetition of the theft in 1990 of the bronze statue of a 1914–18 airman – subsequently replaced by a copy of Butler's Battle of Britain pilot.

Notwithstanding the Club's great art collection, a constant source of interest and indeed inspiration, for many members it is the view along the first floor corridor from the Cowdray Room that most impresses. Here, with the Silver Cabinet in the distance, is displayed the Club's unique collection of squadron and other unit badges, almost twice as many as the 200 originally envisaged in 1937 (p. 30). Even now there remain gaps in the sequence, mainly relating to relatively short-lived squadrons that existed during the Second World War; sometimes a member or more usually a visitor notices one of these and offers to repair the omission, maybe with the help of friends. So the display still expands, albeit very slowly. Here then is the Club's permanent tribute to the Royal Air Force of the past and present, together with a moving reminder of the sheer scale and extent of its world-wide roles in years gone by.

Today's many thousands of members have good reason to be proud of the way the Club has been established and improved over its first 80 years of life at 128 Piccadilly. They appreciate too the quality of the many services it provides and the dedicated work required of its Committee and staff to make it all possible. Perhaps even more significant, they are privileged to be connected with one of the finest reminders to the world at large, here in Central London, of the part played by the Royal Air Force in the nation's history during the twentieth century.

OFFICERS OF THE CLUB

PATRONS

1918–1936	His Majesty King George V
1937–1952	His Majesty King George VI
1952–	Her Majesty Queen Elizabeth II

VICE-PATRONS

1968–1992	Marshal of the Royal Air Force Sir Dermot Boyle
1992–	Air Chief Marshal Sir Lewis Hodges
2002–	Marshal of the Royal Air Force Sir Michael Beetham

PRESIDENTS

1921–1927	The 1st Viscount Cowdray
1928–1935	The 2nd Viscount Cowdray
1936–1944	The 3rd Viscount Cowdray
1945–1967	Marshal of the Royal Air Force Sir John Salmond
1968–1979	Marshal of the Royal Air Force Sir Dermot Boyle
1980–1984	Marshal of the Royal Air Force The Lord Cameron of Balhousie
1985–1992	Air Chief Marshal Sir Lewis Hodges
1992–2002	Marshal of the Royal Air Force Sir Michael Beetham
2002–	Marshal of the Royal Air Force The Lord Craig of Radley

CHAIRMEN

1918	Major General Sefton Brancker
1919–1920	Major General Oliver Swann
1921–1929	Brigadier General R. H. More
1929–1936	Air Commodore W. F. McNeece Foster
1936–1937	Air Marshal Sir Frederick Bowhill
1937–1945	Lieutenant Colonel W. C. Bersey
1945–1948	Air Marshal J. J. Breen
1948–1949	Air Marshal Sir Leslie Hollinghurst
1949–1952	Air Marshal Sir Alan Lees
1952–1953	Air Chief Marshal Sir James Robb
1953–1954	Air Commodore W. P. G. Pretty
1954–1955	Air Vice-Marshal S. R. Ubee

1955–1956	Air Marshal The Earl of Bandon
1956–1957	Air Vice-Marshal M. L. Heath
1957–1960	Air Vice-Marshal J. G. W. Weston
1960–1961	Air Commodore J. H. Searby
1961–1963	Air Vice-Marshal P. T. Philpott
1963–1964	Air Commodore A. V. R. Johnstone
1964–1965	Air Marshal Sir Walter Pretty
1965–1967	Air Commodore N. Cameron
1967–1970	Air Commodore F. B. Sowrey
1970–1973	Air Commodore B. Hamilton
1973–1975	Air Vice-Marshal R. P. Harding
1975–1977	Air Commodore J. Langston
1977–1982	Air Commodore R. L. Lees
1982–1983	Air Commodore G. J. B. Claridge
1984–1987	Air Commodore R. H. Wood
1987–1989	Air Commodore R. H. Kyle
1989–1990	Air Commodore D. R. Hawkins
1990–1992	Air Commodore D. T. Davies
1992–1994	Air Commodore H. W. Hall
1994–1996	Air Vice-Marshal P. Dodworth
1996–1998	Air Vice-Marshal P. J. Goddard
1998–2000	Air Vice-Marshal K. D. Filbey
2000–2003	Air Vice-Marshal P. W. Roser
2003–	Air Vice-Marshal D. C. C. Couzens

SECRETARIES

1918–1919	Major Morley
1919–1919	Captain Cayley
1919–1920	Captain Groom
1920–1928	Major R. D. Anderson
1928–1929	Captain Wynyard
1930–1937	Group Captain A. B. Burdett
1937–1941	Wing Commander C. P. Ogden
1941–1947	Major C. P. Radclyffe-Dugmore
1947–1952	Squadron Leader E. E. Hardie
1952–1954	Wing Commander S. P. A. Bousfield
1954–1960	Group Captain V. G. A. Bennett
1960–1961	Group Captain J. H. S. Richards
1961–1966	Group Captain A. V. Rogers
1966–1966	Squadron Leader A. J. Hayter
1966–1968	Mr W. A. Jolly
1968–1976	Mr E. A. Jeffreys
1976–1991	Squadron Leader J. Swaffield
1991–	Mr P. N. Owen

THE CLUBHOUSE IN 1924

It is not possible to provide a plan of the Clubhouse's internal arrangements as at its opening in 1922. Throughout the inter-war period there are many tantalising references in the Minutes to 'copies of floor plans attached', but none can be found in the Club Archives. However, a comprehensive inventory for December 1924 of everything in the Club, down to the last chamber pot, has fortunately survived, and this description of the interior in 1924 is based on it. The Clubhouse remained very much as described here until well after the Second World War.

The interior was appointed and furnished in the idiom of the traditional London Club, presenting an image of polished hardwood and leather solidity with little reference to its RAF connections. As one entered via the swing doors from Piccadilly, the marble-floored Entrance Hall set the scene with its open fire, mahogany tables and chairs and, as ornament, two six-inch steel shells and two antelope heads. Ahead stretched the Long Corridor with more mahogany and the walls adorned with a pair of large elephant tusks and nine assorted game heads, stags, antelope and goat.

The location of the principal Public Rooms was dictated by the fact that while ladies were admitted to the Club from the outset they were strictly contained so as not to intrude upon its male ethos. The Ground Floor was the men's exclusive preserve. The Grand Staircase was as it is now (though there was no stairway to the basement). To its right lay the heart of the Club, the Smoking Room. Here, hung near the fireplace, was the portrait of Lord Cowdray. Comprehensively furnished with leather-topped mahogany tables

and newspaper stands, it offered its readers and smokers ample stuffed cowhide comfort in an assortment of Chesterfields, settees, easy chairs and window seats. Heavy green brocade curtains and a Wilton carpet protected by 19 brass ashtrays completed its air of masculine ease. Lord Cowdray and the King and Queen shared a wall space with the heads of ten goats, two antelopes and an Assyrian buffalo; 18 bell-pushes ensured prompt service of drinks. In the Ante-room was to be found 'the Boy in Blue Blouse', the Club's first painting (see p. 133). A much smaller Lounge seated up to 17 in flowered tapestry rather than leather with, by way of ornament, a bronze head of Lord Cowdray and a pair of large elephant tusks.

Leading from the Long Corridor was first the American Bar (now the Cloakroom area) furnished with padded cowhide bar stools, a pair of cowhide settees and occasional tables. On the opposite side of the corridor was the Billiard Room with two billiard tables, and at the far end the Card Room which provided for up to 20 players. As well as more mahogany and stuffed leather, these rooms had between them 13 sets of mounted skulls with horns, seven antelope heads and horns, two buffalo heads and a stuffed tarpon.

The first floor had to compromise, for here were the ladies also. Overlooking Green Park was the Dining Room. The ladies with their male hosts were seated in a screened-off portion, an arrangement which throughout the 'twenties was a constant cause of complaint (in the 'thirties they used the Ballroom). Again all was mahogany and dark blue leather, with seating for 114 at a total of 31 tables ranging in size from one six-foot circular table to 18 36-inch-square tables. Over the fireplaces at each end were large panelled mirrors, each with a sunken electric clock. The curtains were blue tapestry. A further 30 diners could be seated in the Small Dining Room (today's Drawing Room).

On the west side of the first-floor corridor was the members' Reading Room cum Library (originally intended for the Ladies' Lounge), with its mahogany writing tables and chairs, two dark leather Chesterfields and 14 armchairs. On the opposite side lay the Ballroom, which had been furnished by Lady Cowdray in 1923 as the Ladies' Lounge. Here amber damask curtains and a blue figured Wilton carpet set off gilded wicker furniture, 22 glass topped tables, and a mixture of settees and easy chairs with dark blue cushions. Four Cantonese vases and three Chinese figures provided suitable ornamentation, while entertainment was catered for with a mahogany grand pianoforte. Across the corridor lay the Ladies' Drawing Room and Anteroom, containing mahogany and satinwood tables, settees and chairs, and decorated with more Chinese porcelain. All rooms were liberally supplied with ashtrays.

On the next floor was the Mezzanine Suite, used for small, private dinners. This comprised a Dining Room seating ten, an Ante-room in which were displayed the three Running Horse pewter tankards and a small piece of a Zeppelin, and a small Card Room.

The residential amenities reflected the period. Members' bedrooms occupied the second, third and fourth floors, none en suite, but with an average of one bathroom to three bedrooms. Typically the bedrooms provided a wash basin with towel rails, shelves, etc., a three-foot oak bedstead with boxspring mattress, wardrobe, dressing-table and chair – and a chamber cupboard with chamber pot. Some larger rooms also provided a desk. Smoking was permitted in every room. The hot water central heating from coal-fired boilers that warmed the Club's public rooms did not extend to the bedrooms but electric radiators could be hired. Two valet rooms were provided on each floor.

The Secretary – who was expected to be single – was accommodated on the fourth floor. His suite comprised an entrance lobby leading to his sitting room, which was fully furnished with writing desk and chair, settee and easy chair, and heated by an open fire. The bedroom was furnished in the same style as for the members but, as with the sitting room, carpeted in Wilton. He had a bathroom next door, shared with members.

Staff accommodation was situated on the fifth floor, and also in No 4 Park Lane. Spartan to modern eyes, it was undoubtedly comparable with contemporary provision in country and town houses. Rooms were either three-bedded or four-bedded – with on average eight rooms being serviced by two bathrooms. Typical furnishings were 27-inch iron tubular bedsteads with wire mattresses and hair overlay, chests of drawers with swing mirrors, Windsor chairs and chamber pots at one per occupant.

For 20 years after 1945, post-war austerity followed by increasing financial difficulties prevented the Club achieving more than essential maintenance and repairs, although the decision taken in 1955 to transfer the Smoking Room to the first floor overlooking Green Park proved to be one of the most propitious changes to the original lay out. Furnishings and ambiance remained as they had been before the war and it was only the Hodges reforms that enabled the Club's transformation to begin.

THE CLUB LAYOUT

Public Rooms The names on the floor plans indicate their present use. Below each floor plan are listed the changing uses of these rooms insofar as these can be deduced from surviving club records.

GROUND FLOOR

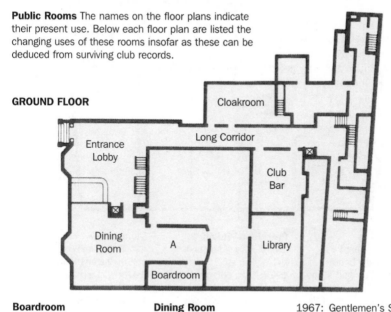

Boardroom
1922: Store
1991: Boardroom (Dining Area)

Club Bar
1922: Billiard Room
1965: Gentlemen's Bar
1989: Club Bar

Dining Room
1922: Smoking Room
1956: Dining Room
A: 1956: Oyster Bar
1967: Incorporated into Dining Room

Library
1922: Card Room
1951: Snack Bar

1967: Gentlemen's Smoking Room
1989: Writing Room
2002: Library

Cloak Room
1922: American Bar
1947: Gentlemen's Cloak Room

BASEMENT

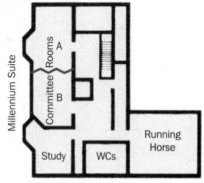

Committee Rooms A and B
1922: Storage Area
1967: Buttery
1970: Buttery/Disco
1974: Buttery
2000: Committee Rooms

Study
1922: Storage Area
1972: Buttery: Grill Area
2000: Study

Running Horse
1922: Storage Area
1978: Running Horse

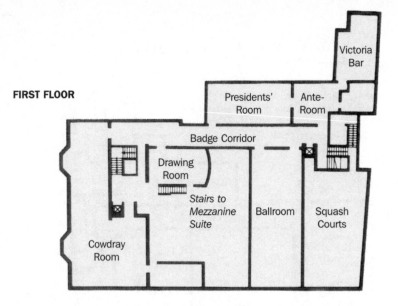

FIRST FLOOR

Cowdray Room
1922: Dining Room
1956: Smoking Room
1967: Club Lounge / Mixed Bar
1968: Cowdray Room and Bar

Drawing Room
1922: Small Dining Room
1927: Quick Lunch Room
193?: Writing Room
1967: Television Room
1982: Drawing Room

Presidents' Room
1920: Planned as Ladies' Lounge
1922: Gentlemen's Writing/ Reading Room
1935: Ladies' Lounge
1969: Drawing Room
1978: Presidents' Room

Ballroom
(Always known as 'Ballroom' notwithstanding varied uses)
1923: Ladies' Lounge
1925: Mixed Dining Room
1945: Function Room

Victoria Bar
1922: Cocktail Bar
1968: Victoria Bar/Disco
1970: Victoria Bar

Mezzanine Suite
Floor plan not shown
1922: Private Dining Suite

Ante-Room
1922: Ladies' Ante-Room
1966: Ante-Room

INDEX